# HARMONY WITHIN: UNLOCKING THE SECRETS OF HOLISTIC WELLNESS

## HOW TO ACHIEVE UNITY OF MIND, BODY, & SPIRIT USING ANCIENT WISDOM AND MODERN PRACTICES

ELLIOTT MIDDLETON PHD

As water reflects the face, so one's life reflects the heart.

— PROVERBS 27:19

# PREFACE

The world has been torn apart in recent years. Pursuing balance and inner peace has become a survival skill. *Harmony Within: Unlocking the Secrets of Holistic Wellness* shares my journey and discoveries in holistic health and spiritual growth, offering a fresh perspective.

My quest for a spiritual approach to surviving our current global turmoil led me on a far-flung expedition. I immersed myself in many cultures and practices that foster overall well-being and dived into the scientific literature supporting ancient wisdom. Each encounter has added to the tapestry of wisdom and experiences I share with you on these pages.

*Harmony Within* is not just a guide; it's a practical tool for personal transformation. It doesn't just uncover the fundamental principles of holistic health, it provides actionable advice for nurturing your body and mind. With specific exercises and meditation practices, it helps align your physical, mental, and spiritual well-being. And it introduces techniques that empower you to maintain this harmony in your daily life. The power to transform yourself is within your reach.

Especially in a world with widespread hunger, it's crucial to remember the significance of every meal. Each bite is a divine blessing. I will repeat this throughout the book, as it is one of the lessons that impacted me the most.

I've poured my heart and soul into the creation of this book. My deepest hope is that these words will ignite a spark within you, inspiring you to embark on your path to self-discovery and inner peace, and that you will find the dedication to see it through. I am profoundly grateful for the many teachers and mentors who have guided me, and I am especially grateful to you, dear reader, for embracing these teachings. Your journey is important to me. May this book serve as a guiding light on your journey to wholeness and serenity.

**Gratefully yours,**

Elliott Middleton, Ph.D.

# INTRODUCTION

Welcome to *Harmony Within: Unlocking the Secrets of Holistic Wellness*. You're not alone if you've ever felt like something is missing—a sense of balance, a deeper connection, a sense of meaning in your day-to-day life. Unprecedented events in recent years have driven us apart and disconnected us from ourselves. To start, this book serves as your guide to understanding how the food you eat and the way you treat your body can affect your spiritual well-being.

## MY JOURNEY

Let's rewind a few years to when I began integrating my diet with spirituality. Like many, I was caught up in the busyness of life and often neglected my health and spiritual practices. It wasn't until I remembered that my father had introduced me to mindful eating years ago that I truly grasped the deep connection between what I consumed and my spiritual well-being.

I remember sitting at my dining table, trying to savor an apple mindfully for the first time. It was a simple exercise but incredibly transformative. I became more present and connected as I focused on the apple's taste, texture, and aroma. This moment of mindfulness revealed a gateway to deeper spiritual awareness, leading me to explore various dietary practices that could enhance my spiritual well-being.

## OVERVIEW OF THE BOOK

This book is designed to guide you through how our bodies and minds affect our spiritual health. We'll explore:

1. **The Unity of Body and Spirit:** Discover the holistic view of well-being that integrates body, mind, and spirit, drawing from ancient traditions and biblical teachings.
2. **Mindful Eating and Spiritual Well-being:** Learn how being present with your food can enhance your spiritual connection.
3. **The Role of Sound Healing:** Explore the ancient practice of sound healing and how it can enhance our mental and spiritual health.
4. **Diet and Mental Health:** Learn about the emerging field of nutritional psychiatry and how certain foods can boost mental and spiritual well-being.
5. **Spiritual Practices and Cancer Treatment:** Learn how integrating diet with spiritual practices can support those undergoing cancer treatment or any other illness.
6. **How Diet Affects the Spiritual Life:** Learn about the spiritual significance of food and

practical guidelines for nourishing both body and spirit.

7. **Integrating Meditation and Diet:** Mindful eating is a form of meditation that leads to a more spiritual experience at the dinner table.
8. **Fasting for Spiritual Well-being:** Explore the spiritual and physical benefits of fasting, supported by modern science and historical and religious perspectives.
9. **The Power of Community:** Learn about the vital role of community support in maintaining dietary and spiritual practices.
10. **Cultural and Traditional Influences:** Gain insights into traditional dietary practices and their spiritual significance worldwide.
11. **The Science of Gratitude and Well-being:** Learn about the psychological benefits of gratitude and its impact on health.
12. **The Connection Between Physical Activity and Spiritual Health:** Understand how regular exercise can enhance spiritual growth.

Each chapter contains practical tips, personal stories, and scientific insights to help you incorporate these practices into your daily life. After reading this book, you will understand how to nourish your body, mind, and spirit to produce integrated, holistic health.

So, grab a cup of tea, settle into a comfortable spot, and embark on this transformative journey towards holistic well-being. Remember, the path to spiritual and physical health is not about perfection but about making mindful choices that honor and nourish your entire being. Let's begin this journey together.

# CHAPTER I

# THE UNITY OF BODY, MIND, AND SPIRIT

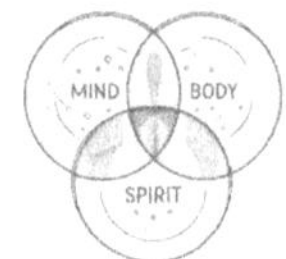

## CONCEPT OF HOLISTIC WELL-BEING

To truly appreciate the unity of body, mind, and spirit, we must reflect on how different traditions and cultures have approached this concept. From ancient Ayurvedic practices in India to Traditional Chinese Medicine, holistic well-being has always been about more than just physical health. It's about achieving harmony within ourselves.

Ayurveda, the ancient Indian system of medicine, is a perfect example. It teaches that health is the balanced and dynamic integration of our environment, body, mind, and spirit. The Ayurvedic diet is tailored to the individual based on their *dosha* (body type) and aims to maintain this balance through specific foods, herbs, and lifestyle practices.

Traditional Chinese Medicine (TCM) also emphasizes balance, particularly the balance of yin and yang and the flow of *qi* (energy) through the body. In TCM, food is seen as medicine, and dietary recommendations are made based on a person's unique constitution and the specific needs of their body and mind.

These traditions offer a comprehensive view of health that goes beyond the physical. They remind us that what we eat can influence our body, mind, and spirit.

## BIBLICAL AND SPIRITUAL FOUNDATIONS

The Bible offers insights into the connection between physical health and spiritual well-being. For instance, 1 Corinthians 6:19-20 (NIV) states, "Do you not know that your bodies are temples of the Holy Spirit, who is in you, whom you have received from God? You are not your own; you were bought at a price. Therefore, honor God with your bodies."

We must treat our bodies with respect and care, as they are sacred vessels integral to our spiritual life. It suggests that caring for our physical health is a personal and spiritual responsibility. Each of us is a spirit in a bodily temple. Solomon, the author of the Book of Ecclesiastes, states that God has planted eternity in the hearts of humankind (Ecclesiastes 3:11). We need to take care of the temple if we are to transition successfully into eternity.

Proverbs 17:22 (NIV) underscores the connection between physical and emotional health: "A cheerful heart is good medicine, but a crushed spirit dries up the bones." Our emotional and spiritual states can directly affect our physical health.

The concept of nourishing body and spirit can be seen in how Jesus taught his disciples about the importance of caring for one's spiritual well-being alongside physical nourishment. In Matthew 4:4 (NIV), Jesus says, "Man shall not live on bread alone, but on every word that comes from the mouth of God." Spiritual nourishment is as essential as physical food. We shall see that it even can program our DNA.

## PRACTICAL STEPS TO HOLISTIC HEALTH

Balancing diet and physical needs with spiritual practices can seem daunting, but it's about making small, consistent changes that honor your physical and spiritual needs. Here are some practical steps to get you started:

**1. Listen to Your Body:** Your body often tells you what it needs. Pay attention to hunger cues, cravings, and how different foods make you feel. This mindfulness can lead to healthier choices that align with your physical and spiritual well-being.

**2. Incorporate Spiritual Practices:** Integrate prayer, Bible reading, affirmations, meditation, and mindfulness into your daily routine. These practices can enhance awareness and connection to your body and its needs. For example, starting your day with a morning prayer or meditation can set a positive tone and help you make mindful choices.

**3. Make Mindful Food Choices:** Choose foods that nourish your body and soul. Opt for whole, unprocessed foods that provide essential nutrients. Consider where your food comes from and how it's prepared. Eating with gratitude and awareness can transform a simple meal into a spiritual experience.

**4. Balance and Moderation:** Balancing your diet and lifestyle is essential. Indulging occasionally is okay, but aim for moderation in all things. This balanced approach can help prevent deprivation and support long-term health and spiritual well-being.

**5. Reflect and Adjust:** Regularly evaluate your diet and

spiritual practices. Are they bringing you joy and fulfillment? Are there areas for improvement? Are you getting enough exercise?

## EXAMPLES OF INTEGRATING HOLISTIC PRACTICES INTO DAILY LIFE

**Morning Rituals:** Start your day with a simple ritual that connects body and soul. This could be a few minutes of meditation, a prayer, or a gratitude journal. Many Christians and Jews have found that reading a chapter from the Book of Proverbs provides a handy daily meditation. Proverbs contains thirty-one brief chapters, so there is one for every day of the month. In addition, the Appendix contains quotations from the Old and New Testaments with suggested meditations.

**Mindful Meals:** Take time to prepare and eat without distractions. Focus on the flavors, textures, and aromas of your food. This mindfulness can enhance your appreciation and connection to what you're eating.

**Physical Activity:** Incorporate physical activity that you enjoy, and that allows you to connect with your body. This could be yoga, walking, or any other exercise that brings you joy and helps you stay grounded. Walking is linked to a lower mortality risk. Research indicates that walking around 7,500 steps per day (approximately 3.75 miles) can significantly reduce the risk of death, providing long-term health benefits and promoting longevity (Harvard Health) (Mayo Clinic).

**Evening Reflection:** Complete your day with a moment of contemplation. Reflect on your day's activities, how they made you feel, and the impact of your spiritual practices on your day. This can aid in making more mindful choices in the future.

By following these steps and integrating holistic practices into your daily life, you can nurture your body, mind, and spirit, creating a harmonious and fulfilling life. Remember, it's about the journey and the small, consistent steps that lead to lasting change. We will explore these in more detail in the following chapters.

# CHAPTER 2

# MINDFUL EATING AND SPIRITUAL WELL-BEING

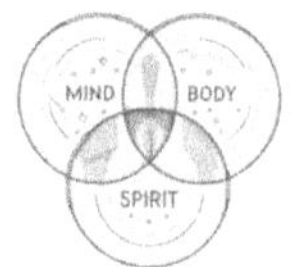



In today's fast-paced world, it's all too easy to eat on autopilot, barely noticing our food's flavors, textures, and smells. We often eat while working, watching TV, or scrolling through our phones. This mindless eating can lead to overconsumption, poor digestion, and a disconnect between our physical and spiritual selves.

## MINDFULNESS AND EATING

Mindful eating is about being fully present during your meals. It involves paying attention to the colors, smells, textures, flavors, temperatures, and even the sounds of your food. It's about observing how your body feels before, during, and after eating. Are you eating because you're hungry, bored, or stressed? How does the food taste? How does it make you feel afterward?

This practice is rooted in mindfulness, a meditation technique focusing on the present moment. Jon Kabat-Zinn, a pioneer in mindfulness, describes it as "paying attention in a particular way: on purpose, in the present moment, and nonjudgmentally" (Kabat-Zinn, 1994). When applied to eating, this mindfulness can transform a mundane activity into a deeply spiritual practice.

## BENEFITS OF BEING PRESENT WITH YOUR FOOD

Mindful eating offers numerous benefits for physical and spiritual well-being. On a physical level, it can lead to better digestion, improved portion control, and greater meal satisfaction. When you're fully present, you're more likely to notice your body's hunger and fullness cues, helping you eat the right amount of food for your needs.

Spiritually, mindful eating can enhance your connection to the food you eat and the act of eating itself. It encourages gratitude for your food's nourishment and fosters a deeper appreciation for the efforts that go into growing, harvesting, and preparing it. This practice can transform meals into opportunities for reflection, gratitude, and connection with the divine.

## PRACTICAL TECHNIQUES

Ready to give it a try? Here are some practical techniques to help you get started:

**1. Savoring an Apple:** As my father taught me, take an apple and examine it closely. Notice its color, shape, and texture. Smell it and appreciate its fragrance. Take a small bite and let it sit in your mouth before chewing slowly. Pay attention to the flavors and textures as you chew.

**2. Chewing Thoroughly:** Aim to chew each bite of food 20-30 times. This slows your eating pace and allows you to experience your food's flavors and textures fully. It also aids digestion by breaking down food more thoroughly.

**3. Eliminating Distractions:** Turn off the TV, put away your phone, and focus solely on your meal. Create a calm, pleasant environment for eating. This helps you stay present and fully engage with the experience of eating.

**4. Listening to Your Body:** Pay attention to your body's hunger and fullness signals. Eat when you're hungry and stop when you're satisfied—or almost satisfied. This can prevent overeating and help you develop a healthier relationship with food.

## CASE STUDY: MARGARET'S TRANSFORMATION

Consider Margaret, a busy professional who often found herself eating on the go. Her meals were usually consumed before a computer screen or in the car between meetings. Margaret struggled with digestive issues and often felt disconnected from her body and her faith.

After learning about mindful eating, Margaret decided to try it. She started by setting aside time each day for a quiet, undisturbed meal. She chose simple, nourishing foods and practiced savoring each bite. Over time, Margaret noticed significant improvements in her digestion and overall well-being. She felt more connected to her food and more grateful for the nourishment it provided. This newfound mindfulness also enhanced her spiritual life, as she began to see mealtime as an opportunity for reflection and gratitude.

## SPIRITUAL INSIGHTS FROM MINDFUL EATING

Viewing eating as a spiritual practice can transform your relationship with food. Here are some spiritual insights to consider:

**1. Gratitude:** Before each meal, give thanks for the food you're about to eat. Reflect on the journey to reach your plate and the people who made it possible. This practice can foster a deep gratitude and connection to the world around you. In Chapter 11, we will consider the science of gratitude.

**2. Connection:** Eating mindfully can help you feel more connected to your body and its needs. You can develop a healthier, more intuitive relationship with food by focusing on hunger and fullness cues.

**3. Presence:** Being fully present during meals can enhance your awareness and appreciation for eating. It can turn a simple meal into a moment of mindfulness and spiritual reflection.

**4. Compassion:** Mindful eating can cultivate compassion for yourself and others. By listening to your body's needs and making thoughtful food choices, you're practicing self-care and honoring the body God has given you.

## PRACTICAL TIPS FOR CULTIVATING MINDFUL EATING

**1. Start Small:** Begin by incorporating mindful eating into one daily meal. As you become more comfortable with the practice, you can gradually extend it to other meals.

**2. Create a Ritual:** Establish a pre-meal ritual to help you transition into a mindful eating mindset. This could be a short prayer, a moment of silence, or a few deep breaths.

**3. Use All Your Senses:** Engage all your senses during meals. Notice the colors, smells, textures, and flavors of your food. Listen to the sounds of eating and savor the experience.

**4. Reflect:** Take a moment after each meal to reflect on the experience. How did the food taste? How did it make you feel? What did you notice about your hunger and fullness cues?

# AFTERWORD

Mindful eating is a spiritual practice that can enhance your connection to your food, body, and the divine. Being fully present during meals can transform eating into a sacred experience, fostering gratitude, connection, and compassion. So, the next time you sit down to eat, take a moment to slow down, savor each bite, and appreciate the nourishment your food provides.

# CHAPTER 3

# THE ROLE OF SOUND HEALING

Sound healing may sound like something out of a science fiction novel, but it's an ancient practice with roots in various cultures worldwide. From the guttural buzzing of the monks of Tibet to the drumming circles of Native American tribes to the chanting of Gregorian monks, sound has long been used for healing and spiritual growth. Today, science is beginning to catch up with what these traditions have known for centuries: sound can impact our physical, mental, and spiritual well-being.

## INTRODUCTION TO SOUND HEALING

Sound healing involves using specific tones, frequencies, and rhythms to promote healing and well-being. This can be achieved through music, singing bowls, tuning forks, singing, chanting, and even modern technologies like binaural beats. Sound can influence the vibrational frequencies of our bodies and minds, bringing them into a state of harmony and balance. Modern physics teaches that our bodies are a collection of vibrating subatomic strings, just like a violin!

One of the most well-known instruments used in sound healing is the Tibetan singing bowl. Traditionally made from a mix of metals, these bowls produce a rich, resonant sound when struck or circled with a mallet. The vibrations from the bowl can penetrate deep into the body, promoting relaxation and healing on a cellular level.

## SCIENTIFIC BASIS FOR SOUND HEALING

While the spiritual and anecdotal benefits of sound healing are well-documented, modern science is also beginning to explore its potential. Studies have shown that sound can influence our brainwaves, promoting relaxation and focus. For example, binaural beats—a form of sound therapy that uses two slightly different frequencies played in each ear— have been found to reduce anxiety and improve mood (Goyal et al., 2014). You can find many binaural beat tracks on YouTube. In some experiments, brainwaves synchronized across both brain hemispheres, inducing a state of deep tranquillity.

Research also suggests that sound healing can have tangible effects on the body. A British Academy of Sound Therapy study found that participants who underwent sound therapy reported significant reductions in stress, anxiety, and physical pain (Goldsby et al., 2016). The vibrations from sound can stimulate the body's natural healing processes, improving circulation, reducing inflammation, and promoting overall well-being.

However, the importance of frequency has recently been demonstrated in a series of experiments relating vibrational frequency—whether electromagnetic or acoustic—to the behavior of DNA!

Russian physicist Peter Garyaev and Nobel Prize winner Luc Montagnier demonstrated that electromagnetic or sound frequencies can "tune" and even recreate our DNA.

Montagnier conducted an experiment in which he captured the electromagnetic emissions of DNA in a beaker, converted them into a "sound" file, and transmitted them to another location. Upon broadcasting these electromagnetic frequencies into a solution, the DNA reassembled itself in a solution of proteins.

It would seem that DNA is an antenna, and it responds differently to the various vibrational frequencies it is exposed to.

Garyaev's experiments suggest that acoustic and electromagnetic frequencies can "tune" DNA. In one experiment, he beamed microwaves through tissue samples of one species onto developing embryos of another, resulting in the developing embryos acquiring some of the characteristics of the first species.

Garyaev also found that simply reproducing the electromagnetic frequencies his instruments picked up from particularly healthy DNA as sound, when played for an infirm patient, could "tune" the patient's DNA to eliminate the infirmity. Some of Garyaev's original sound files, such as "Wave Immunity," can be found on YouTube. Our DNA appears to be like a tuning fork and will resonate with frequencies presented to it, even acoustically.

Garyaev also discovered that the structure of DNA follows language laws. He believed the Holy Scripture could optimally tune our DNA simply by being read or heard (Garyaev, 2013). Ancient Christian writings state, "In the beginning was the Word, and the Word was with God, and the Word was God" (John 1:1 NIV). This ancient wisdom accords with a modern physics view that the substrate of all Being is consciousness and that the world we see is created out of invisible dimensions (Radin 1997).

Each of us is a collection of vibrating strings from the invisible quantum realm. At the quantum level, everything in the Universe is instantaneously interconnected. Radin's famous experiments demonstrate that our subconscious minds attuned to "the field" are aware of events before they happen, violating the classical laws of physics.

The Bible offers ancient wisdom on this topic (Hebrews 11:1-6 NIV):

*Now faith is confidence in what we hope for and assurance about what we do not see.*

*This is what the ancients were commended for.*

*By faith we understand that the universe was formed at God's command, so that what is seen was not made out of what was visible.*

The writer of Hebrews asserts that there is an entire realm beyond the visible physical world, out of which the physical world was made. This realm might correspond to the invisible subatomic quantum realm, the "quantum foam" from which particles appear and disappear. That realm might very well be the consciousness of God.

We must cultivate our awareness of spiritual dimensions, as the ancients did. The world is not made of visible substances. The frequency and spiritual truth of the images, ideas, and language we expose ourselves to will determine how we resonate. We will return to this topic in Chapter 12.

*"More and more, the universe resembles a thought."*
— Sir James Jeans, British physicist

## BENEFITS OF CLASSICAL MUSIC

Listening to classical music has been associated with various cognitive benefits. One well-known effect is the "Mozart effect," which suggests that listening to Mozart's music can temporarily enhance spatial-temporal reasoning abilities (Jaušovec & Habe 2003). While walking, I sometimes enjoy listening to classical music through wired earbuds (so as not to irradiate my brain with wireless earbuds). The walk becomes a meditative dance. Other times, I enjoy listening to the birds.

Listening to classical music has been found to have several positive effects on health and well-being. One study indicates that classical music can modulate ("tune") genes responsible for brain functions, promoting neuroplasticity and improving cognitive abilities (Kanduri et al., 2015). This is a remarkable result. Additionally, Harvard Medical School reports that music therapy, including listening to classical music, can reduce stress, lower blood pressure, and improve mood by triggering the release of dopamine, a feel-good neurotransmitter (Harvard Medical School, 2015).

## IMPACT ON SPIRITUAL WELL-BEING

Sound healing goes beyond physical health and impacts our mental and spiritual well-being. Making or listening to sound can be a deeply meditative experience that helps quiet the mind and connect with a higher state of consciousness. Many individuals discover that sound healing sessions leave them feeling more centered, grounded, and spiritually connected.

One powerful aspect of sound healing is its ability to facilitate deep states of meditation. Music's repetitive, rhythmic nature can help quiet the mind and promote inner peace. This is particularly true for practices like chanting and drumming, which have been used for centuries to induce trance-like states and enhance spiritual awareness, and for rhythmic music. Communal singing is part of the worship practices of virtually all religions.

## PERSONAL ANECDOTES AND TESTIMONIALS

Sound healing has changed people's lives. Consider Mark, a person with anorexia who dealt with anxiety for many years and attempted various treatments, including medication and talk therapy, with little success. It wasn't until he came across a local sound healing circle that he experienced true relief. The first time he participated in the circle, surrounded by the harmonious sounds of singing bowls and gongs, he felt a deep calm. He was able to eat a full dinner that night. Regular sound healing sessions helped Mark manage his anxiety more effectively than anything else he had tried.

In another case, Priscilla used sound healing to aid her recovery from a kidney transplant. During her treatment, Priscilla attended weekly sound healing sessions. She found that the vibrations from the singing bowls helped alleviate her pain and fatigue, and the meditative aspect of the sessions provided her with a much-needed sense of peace and hope. Priscilla credits sound healing with not only aiding her physical recovery but also helping her maintain a positive and resilient mindset.

## INTEGRATING SOUND HEALING WITH DIET

Combining sound healing with mindful eating can amplify the benefits of both practices. Imagine starting your meal with a few minutes of sound healing, using a singing bowl or a simple sung grace to create a calm and centered atmosphere. This can help you transition into a state of mindfulness, allowing you to appreciate the flavors and textures of your food thoroughly.

Here are some practical tips for integrating sound healing with your mealtime routines:

**1. Pre-Meal Ritual:** Before eating, listen to calming sounds, such as Tibetan singing bowls or your favorite tranquil music. Or sing a grace, as many people used to do in childhood. This can help you transition from the busyness of the day into a more mindful state.

**2. Mindful Chewing:** As you eat, focus on the sounds of your meal. Notice the crunch of vegetables, the sound of your fork against the plate, or the gentle glass clinking. This can enhance your sensory experience and deepen your connection to eating.

**3. Gratitude and Reflection:** Use sound as a tool for gratitude. At the end of your meal, take a moment to reflect on the nourishment you've received. You might even use a small bell or chime to signal the end of the meal, marking it as a sacred experience.

## CASE STUDY: MARK'S JOURNEY

A highly successful serial entrepreneur, Mark had always been a high-strung alpha male, constantly stressed and anxious about his job and personal life. Medication and talk therapy provided some relief but didn't address the root of his discomfort, and he didn't like being medicated.

A friend invited Mark to a sound healing session. Skeptical but curious, he decided to give it a try. The session involved a combination of Tibetan singing bowls, gongs, and guided meditation. As the sounds filled the room, Mark felt a deep sense of relaxation he had never experienced before. The vibrations seemed to penetrate his body, melting away the tension and stress.

Inspired by this experience, Mark began attending weekly sound healing sessions and incorporating sound healing into his daily routine, using a small singing bowl at home. Over time, Mark noticed significant improvements in his anxiety levels and, with his doctor's permission, stopped his medication.

He felt more centered, present, and connected to his spiritual self. Sound healing not only helped him manage his anxiety but also opened up new pathways for spiritual growth and self-awareness. He began to read the Bhagavad Gita and booked a visit to an ashram in India.


## SPIRITUAL INSIGHTS FROM SOUND HEALING

Sound healing can be a powerful tool for spiritual growth. Here are some spiritual insights that can be gained from this practice:

**1. Harmony and Balance**: Sound healing teaches us the importance of harmony and balance. Just as different frequencies can create a harmonious sound, we can strive to balance other aspects of our lives to create inner harmony.

**2. Presence and Mindfulness:** Engaging with sound healing encourages us to be present and mindful. This practice can help quiet the mind and create a more immediate connection to the present moment and the divine.

**3. Healing and Transformation:** Sound can heal and transform. By incorporating sound healing into our lives, we can facilitate physical, emotional, and spiritual healing, leading to personal growth and transformation.

**4. Connection to the Divine:** Our DNA resonates with language and frequency. Sound healing enhances your connection to the divine. Creating or listening to sound can be a form of prayer or meditation, helping us connect with a higher power and gain spiritual insights. It is essential to be aware of the effect different frequencies have on you.

## PRACTICAL TIPS FOR USING SOUND HEALING

**1. Find What Resonates:** Experiment with different types of sound healing to find what resonates with you. This could be Christian praise music, classical music, singing bowls, tuning forks, chanting, or listening to calming ambient New Age music.

**2. Create a Routine:** Incorporate sound healing into your daily routine. This could be a morning meditation with a singing bowl, a mid-day break with binaural beats, or an evening relaxation session with praise or classical music. The TuneIn app and others allow one to listen to great classical music stations anywhere worldwide, like WQXR from New York or KUSC from Los Angeles.

**3. Combine with Other Practices:** Integrate sound healing with spiritual practices, such as prayer, meditation, or mindful eating. The Psalms were sung in ancient times and in some Christian churches today. Try singing a psalm or a prayer with your melody. David sang and danced in the Old Testament to honor the Lord in many situations.

**4. Attend a Session:** If you desire professional treatment, attend a sound healing session with a trained practitioner. This can provide a more enlightening experience and help you learn how to use sound healing effectively. There are several types of sound therapy, so you must research your choice thoroughly.

Integrating sound healing into your daily routine can enhance your physical, emotional, and spiritual well-being. Whether you're looking to reduce stress, improve your mental health, or deepen your spiritual practice, sound healing offers a powerful tool for nurturing both body and soul. Take a moment to listen, feel, and connect with sound's healing power.

# CHAPTER 4

# DIET AND MENTAL HEALTH

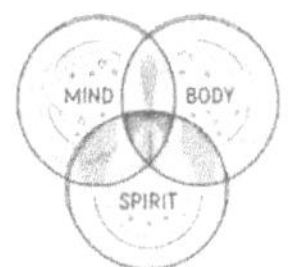


The saying "you are what you eat" has been around for centuries, and it turns out that it holds more truth than we might have imagined. In recent years, the field of nutritional psychiatry has emerged, providing evidence that our diet significantly impacts our mental health. The food we consume can either support our mental well-being or contribute to the development of mental health issues such as depression and anxiety. Let's explore how diet influences mental health, the essential nutrients that play a role, and practical dietary recommendations to boost your mental and spiritual health.

## NUTRITIONAL PSYCHIATRY

Nutritional psychiatry explores the impact of specific foods and nutrients on brain function and mood, as well as the potential use of dietary interventions in preventing and treating mental health disorders. Researchers in this field have determined that a poor diet, characterized by high consumption of processed foods and low intake of essential nutrients, is linked to a higher risk of depression, anxiety, and other mental health issues (Jacka et al., 2017).

A diet with plenty of whole foods, such as fruits, vegetables, whole grains, and lean proteins, has been associated with improved mental health. These foods offer essential nutrients that support brain function, including vitamins, minerals, antioxidants, and healthy fats. Let's explore some of these crucial nutrients.

## CRITICAL NUTRIENTS FOR MENTAL AND SPIRITUAL HEALTH

**1. Omega-3 Fatty Acids:** Omega-3 fatty acids, found in fatty fish (like salmon and mackerel), walnuts, flaxseeds, and chia seeds, are crucial for brain health. These healthy fats have anti-inflammatory properties and support cognitive function and emotional well-being. Studies have shown that omega-3 supplementation can reduce symptoms of depression and anxiety (Freeman et al., 2011).

**2. Leafy Greens:** Leafy greens such as spinach, kale, and Swiss chard are packed with nutrients like folate, magnesium, and iron, essential for brain health. Scientific research has demonstrated a link between folate deficiency and depression. Folate, a B vitamin, is critical for proper brain function. Studies suggest that low levels of folate in the body can impair the synthesis of neurotransmitters such as serotonin, which are crucial for mood regulation.

One study published in the *British Medical Journal* found that folate deficiency is widespread among individuals with depression, and addressing this deficiency can potentially improve depressive symptoms (Reynolds, 2002). Another meta-analysis highlighted that individuals with depression often have lower folate levels compared to those without depression, further supporting the association between folate status and mental health (Gilbody et al., 2007).

**3. Probiotics:** The connection between the gut and the brain is an intriguing area of study that shows how gut health affects mental well-being. Probiotics, which can be found in fermented foods such as yogurt, kefir, sauerkraut, and kimchi, play a role in maintaining a healthy gut microbiome. A balanced gut microbiome supports the production of neurotransmitters like serotonin, which helps regulate mood and anxiety (Sarkar et al., 2016). Most pharmacies stock probiotic capsules containing bacteria from the *Lactobacillus* and *Bifidobacterium* genera and others, essential for gut health. I take a probiotic with six different strains of bacteria!

**4. Antioxidants:** Antioxidants, which are found in colorful fruits and vegetables such as berries, citrus fruits, and bell peppers, protect the brain from oxidative stress and inflammation. This protection is crucial for maintaining cognitive function and mental well-being. Taking 1000 mg of Vitamin C capsules is a great way to increase your Vitamin C levels. Additionally, Carbon-60 (C60) supplements in various oils are potent antioxidants.

**5. B and D Vitamins:** B vitamins such as B6, B12, and folate are crucial for brain health as they assist in producing and regulating neurotransmitters, which play a vital role in regulating mood. Vitamin D3, a hormone, is essential for supporting the immune system. Deficiency in these vitamins can lead to symptoms of depression, anxiety, and illness.

Scientific studies have shown that low levels of Vitamin D3 are associated with an increased risk of contracting respiratory infections, including the flu and COVID-19. For example, a study published in the *Archives of Internal Medi-*

*cine* reported that individuals with lower Vitamin D levels had a higher incidence of upper respiratory tract infections. The study analyzed data from nearly 19,000 participants and found that those with Vitamin D levels below ten ng/mL were more likely to report recent infections than those with higher levels (Ginde, Mansbach & Camargo, 2009).

Additionally, an umbrella review published in *Antioxidants* journal found that low Vitamin D3 levels were significantly associated with increased severity and mortality risk from COVID-19. The review highlighted that Vitamin D3 supplementation could reduce infection severity and improve outcomes for COVID-19 patients (Rea et al., 2023).

Spending time outdoors is the best way to maintain healthy Vitamin D levels. Unfortunately, most people do not, and as a result, suffer from Vitamin D deficiency. Many doctors recommend supplementing with 1000 IU of Vitamin D3 daily.

Regular intake of a balanced multivitamin can also contribute to overall well-being, enhancing quality of life by supporting various bodily functions and improving health outcomes.

**6. Protein:** Protein provides the building blocks for neurotransmitters crucial for brain function. Lean proteins, such as lean beef, poultry, fish, beans, and legumes, provide amino acids that support mental health.

## DIETARY RECOMMENDATIONS

Incorporating these essential nutrients into your diet can help support mental and spiritual health. Here are some practical dietary recommendations:

**1. Eat a Rainbow:** Include a variety of colorful fruits

and vegetables in your meals. Each color represents different antioxidants and nutrients that benefit your brain.

**2. Choose Whole Foods:** Opt for whole, unprocessed foods over processed ones. Whole foods retain their natural nutrients and are free from additives that can negatively impact your health. Choose organic produce.

**3. Incorporate Healthy Fats:** Add sources of omega-3 fatty acids to your diet, such as fatty fish, walnuts, flaxseeds, and chia seeds. Olive oil is also a source of healthy fats. Make your salad dressings with extra-virgin olive oil and vinegar of some variety: balsamic for a sharp flavor and white wine vinegar for a milder taste. A half teaspoon of olive oil a day has been shown to protect brain health in a multi-decade study of 92,000 US adults' nutritional habits, reducing the risk of dementia-related death by 28 percent (Tessier et al., 2024). I put half a teaspoon of C60 in olive oil in my coffee in the morning—not for everyone, I admit.

**4. Include Probiotics:** Incorporate fermented foods into your diet to support gut health and, in turn, mental health. Fermented foods are rich in probiotics, beneficial bacteria supporting gut health. Here are some examples of fermented foods that include probiotics:

**1. Yogurt:** Made from milk fermented by lactic acid bacteria, yogurt is a popular source of probiotics, particularly *Lactobacillus* and *Bifidobacterium* strains.

**2. Kefir:** A fermented milk drink containing diverse bacteria and yeast, kefir is known for its high probiotic content and potential health benefits.

**3. Sauerkraut:** Fermented cabbage that is rich in Lacto-bacillus bacteria; sauerkraut is a traditional food that provides probiotics and is also high in vitamins C and K.

**4. Kimchi:** A Korean dish made from fermented vegetables, usually cabbage and radishes, seasoned with various spices. Kimchi contains probiotics such as Lactobacillus kimchi and other lactic acid bacteria.

**5. Tempeh:** A fermented soybean product that forms a firm, cake-like structure. Tempeh contains probiotics and is a good source of protein, vitamins, and minerals.

**6. Miso:** A Japanese seasoning made by fermenting soybeans with salt and koji (a type of fungus). Miso contains probiotics and is commonly used in soups and marinades.

**7. Kombucha:** A fermented tea drink made using a symbiotic culture of bacteria and yeast (SCOBY). Kombucha is known for its probiotic content and refreshing taste.

**8. Pickles (Fermented):** Cucumbers fermented in a brine (salt water) solution, rather than vinegar, develop beneficial bacteria. Traditional dill pickles are a good example.

**9. Natto:** A traditional Japanese food made from fermented soybeans. Natto contains *Bacillus subtilis* and is known for its intense flavor and sticky texture.

**10. Buttermilk (Traditional):** The liquid left after churning butter from cultured cream. Traditional buttermilk contains probiotics, though many commercial versions do not.

**11. Sourdough Bread:** Made from dough fermented using naturally occurring *lactobacilli* and wild yeast, sourdough bread contains probiotics, especially in the crust.

**12. Fermented Cheese:** Certain types of aged cheeses like Gouda, cheddar, and Swiss can contain probiotics, particularly if they are labeled as containing live cultures.

**13. Fermented Soy Sauce:** Traditional soy sauce, which is made through a fermentation process involving soybeans, wheat, salt, and specific strains of mold, yeast, and bacteria.

Due to their probiotic content, including these fermented foods in your diet can help enhance gut health, improve digestion, and boost overall well-being. Moreover, you should:

- **Stay Hydrated:** Drinking plenty of water is essential for overall health, including brain function. Aim for at least eight glasses of water a day.
- **Limit Sugar and Processed Foods:** High sugar intake and processed foods have been linked to increased inflammation and mental health issues. Reducing your intake of these foods can support better mental health. Alcohol should be avoided or used in moderation.

## CASE STUDY: ELIZABETH'S JOURNEY

Elizabeth's story is a testament to the power of diet in transforming mental health. The daughter of alcoholics, she struggled with depression and anxiety for years. Despite trying various medications and therapies, she couldn't find lasting relief. Her turning point came when she stumbled upon the field of nutritional psychiatry and decided to overhaul her diet.

Elizabeth began by eliminating processed foods and sugars from her diet. She ate more fruits, vegetables, lean proteins, and healthy fats. She also started taking a daily probiotic supplement and increased her intake of omega-3-rich foods. Within a few weeks, Elizabeth noticed significant improvements in her mood and energy levels. Her anxiety decreased, and she felt more emotionally stable.

Over time, Elizabeth's mental health continued to improve. She felt more connected to her body and mind and less haunted by her unhappy childhood. She joined a neighborhood Bible study. The dietary changes supported her mental health and enhanced her overall well-being. Elizabeth's journey exemplifies how nutritional interventions can transform mental health and spiritual well-being.

## SPIRITUAL INSIGHTS FROM DIETARY CHANGES

Viewing dietary changes as acts of self-care and spiritual growth can deepen their impact. Here are some spiritual insights to consider:

**1. Nourishing the Body as a Sacred Act:** Treating your body with respect and care by choosing nourishing foods is honoring the temple of your spirit, and of the Holy Spirit that Christ sent to be with us after his departure. This perspective can transform your relationship with food.

**2. Mindful Eating as a Spiritual Practice:** Once you have modified your diet to be healthier, incorporating mindfulness into your eating habits can enhance your spiritual well-being. Being present with your food can cultivate gratitude, awareness, and a deeper connection to the divine.

**3. Gratitude for Nourishment:** Giving thanks for your food and its nourishment can transform mealtime into a sacred experience. As we'll see in Chapter 12, it may even change the chemistry of your food!

# AFTERWORD

The connection between diet and mental health is not just a theory. It's an important reality. The emerging field of nutritional psychiatry offers valuable insights into how our dietary choices can bolster our mental and spiritual well-being. By incorporating essential nutrients, opting for whole foods, and embracing mindful eating, we can nourish our bodies and minds, fostering a deeper and more meaningful connection to Spirit.

Your diet is not just a passive factor in your mental health but a powerful tool for unlocking your potential. By reframing dietary changes as acts of self-care and spiritual growth, we can take control of our overall well-being and supercharge it.

# CHAPTER 5

# SPIRITUAL PRACTICES AND CANCER TREATMENT

When people receive a challenging diagnosis like cancer, they often find solace and inner strength not just in medical treatments but also in their spiritual beliefs. Linking diet with spiritual practices nurtures both the physical and spiritual aspects of healing. In this section, we present evidence highlighting the importance of spiritual practices in cancer treatment, the benefits of a diet rich in nutrients, and compelling case studies of individuals who have combined these approaches to achieve better outcomes.

## PSYCHOSOCIAL-SPIRITUAL INTERVENTIONS

Cancer treatment is not just a physical battle; it's also an emotional and spiritual journey. Psychosocial-spiritual interventions aim to address the emotional, social, and spiritual needs of patients undergoing cancer treatment. These interventions can include counseling, support groups, prayer, meditation, and mindfulness practices.

Research has shown that patients who engage in spiritual practices often experience better emotional well-being, reduced anxiety, and enhanced hope and purpose (Goyal et al., 2014). Prayer and meditation, in particular, have been found to reduce stress and improve the quality of life for cancer patients. These practices provide a sense of connection to a higher power and a framework for finding meaning and purpose amid illness.

## ROLE OF DIET IN ENHANCING THESE INTERVENTIONS

A nutrient-rich diet is crucial in supporting the body during cancer treatment. Proper nutrition can help boost the immune system, maintain body weight, and enhance the body's healing ability. Certain foods have cancer-fighting properties and can support overall health and well-being.

**Antioxidant-Rich Foods:** Foods high in antioxidants, such as berries, dark leafy greens, and nuts, help combat oxidative stress and inflammation, common during cancer treatment. Antioxidants protect cells from damage and support the body's natural healing processes.

**Protein:** Adequate protein intake is essential for maintaining muscle mass and strength, especially during cancer treatment. Lean proteins, such as chicken, fish, beans, and legumes, are necessary for repair and recovery.

**Hydration:** Staying hydrated is vital for overall health and can help alleviate some side effects of cancer treatment, such as fatigue and nausea. Drinking plenty of water, herbal teas, and broths can support hydration.

**Anti-Inflammatory Foods:** Foods with anti-inflammatory properties, such as turmeric, ginger, and fatty fish, can help reduce inflammation. Inflammation is common during cancer treatment; managing it can improve overall well-being.

**Avoid sugar:** A diet high in sugar has been linked to an increased risk of developing cancer and the progression of existing cancers. This connection is supported by various studies and reviews highlighting several mechanisms by which high sugar intake can contribute to cancer (Peiying & Lorenzo, 2022).

**Fasting:** Fasting has shown potential benefits in cancer treatment by making cancer cells more vulnerable to therapies while protecting normal cells. Research indicates that fasting can reduce insulin growth factor (IGF-1) levels, enhance autophagy (cellular housekeeping), and improve the efficacy of chemotherapy and other treatments. For instance, studies from Cedars-Sinai highlight that fasting can help manage treatment toxicities and possibly improve outcomes in cancer patients (Cedars-Sinai, 2024).

## CASE STUDIES OF INTEGRATING DIET AND SPIRITUAL PRACTICES

Let's examine some inspiring stories from the literature about individuals who have combined spiritual practices with dietary changes to support cancer treatment.

**CASE STUDY: Anna's Journey with Prayer and Nutrition**

Anna was diagnosed with breast cancer at the age of 45. Along with conventional treatments like surgery and chemotherapy, Anna turned to her faith and nutrition to support her healing journey. She incorporated daily prayer and meditation into her routine, finding solace and strength in her spiritual practices.

Anna also made significant changes to her diet. She eliminated processed foods and sugars, focusing on whole foods rich in antioxidants and anti-inflammatory properties. Her meals included fresh fruits and vegetables, lean proteins, and healthy fats. She also stayed hydrated by drinking herbal teas and water throughout the day.

Over time, Anna noticed improvements in her energy levels, mood, and overall well-being. Her spiritual practices gave her peace and purpose, while her nutrient-rich diet supported her body's healing processes. Anna's holistic approach helped her navigate the challenges of cancer treatment with resilience and hope.

CASE STUDY: **Richard's Battle with Colon Cancer**

Richard was diagnosed with colon cancer at the age of 50. Determined to fight the disease with everything he had, Richard sought the guidance of a nutritionist and a spiritual counselor. His nutritionist recommended a diet rich in fiber, antioxidants, and lean proteins, while his spiritual counselor encouraged him to practice daily meditation and gratitude.

Richard followed a plant-based diet, incorporating many fruits, vegetables, whole grains, and legumes. He also included foods known for their anti-cancer properties, such as turmeric, garlic, and green tea. His spiritual practice involved daily meditation, focusing on positive affirmations and visualizing his body healing.

Richard's holistic approach supported his physical health and gave him a sense of empowerment and control over his treatment. He found that meditation helped reduce his anxiety and improve his outlook on life. His journey highlighted the powerful connection between diet, spirituality, and healing.

## PRACTICAL TIPS FOR INTEGRATING DIET AND SPIRITUAL PRACTICES IN CANCER TREATMENT

Here are some practical tips for combining diet and spiritual practices to support cancer treatment:

**1. Start with Small Changes:** Include small changes in your diet and spiritual practices. Gradually increase the frequency and duration of these practices as you become more comfortable.

**2. Create a Routine:** Establish a daily routine that includes time for prayer and meditation. Consistency is critical to reaping the benefits of these practices.

**3. Seek Support:** Reach out to support groups, counselors, or nutritionists who can provide guidance and encouragement. Surrounding yourself with a supportive community can significantly impact your healing journey.

**4. Listen to Your Body:** How your body responds to different foods and spiritual practices. Make adjustments as needed to ensure you are supporting your physical and emotional well-being.

**5. Stay Hydrated:** Drink plenty of water and herbal teas. Proper hydration is essential for overall health and can help alleviate some of the side effects of cancer treatment.

**6. Incorporate Gratitude:** Practice gratitude daily by reflecting on the positive aspects of your life and treatment. This can enhance your spiritual well-being and provide hope and purpose.

## SPIRITUAL INSIGHTS FROM CANCER TREATMENT

Cancer treatment is a challenging journey that can also be an opportunity for spiritual growth. Here are some spiritual insights that can be gained from this experience:

**1. Resilience and Strength:** Facing a severe illness can reveal inner strengths and resilience you never knew you had. Spiritual practices can provide a foundation of support and encouragement during difficult times.

**2. Connection to the Divine:** Many individuals find that their connection to the divine deepens during illness. Prayer, meditation, and other spiritual practices can enhance this connection and provide comfort and guidance.

**3. Gratitude and Presence:** Illness often brings a heightened awareness of the present moment and a greater appreciation for life's simple joys. Practicing gratitude can enhance this awareness and create a sense of peace.

**4. Purpose and Meaning:** Finding meaning and purpose amid illness can be a powerful motivator for healing. Spiritual practices can help you explore and understand the deeper purpose of your journey.

# AFTERWORD

Integrating diet and spiritual practices into cancer treatment provides a holistic approach that supports the physical and spiritual aspects of healing. By incorporating nutrient-rich foods, practicing mindfulness, and engaging in spiritual practices, you can enhance your overall well-being and navigate the challenges of cancer treatment with strength and resilience.

# CHAPTER 6

# HOW DIET AFFECTS THE SPIRITUAL LIFE

Our relationship with food is deeply personal and spiritual. Throughout history, various cultures and religions have recognized the sacred nature of food and its impact on our spiritual well-being. From biblical teachings to modern spiritual practices, we learn that food can nourish our bodies and souls. In this chapter, we will explore the spiritual significance of food, practical guidelines for choosing foods that nourish both body and soul, and the miraculous power of dietary changes on our spiritual lives.

## SPIRITUAL SIGNIFICANCE OF FOOD

Food has always held a sacred place in human culture and spirituality. In many religious traditions, food is more than just sustenance; it symbolizes divine provision and a means of connecting with the sacred. Olive oil is mentioned so often in the Old Testament that it seems to have been considered a divine food by the ancient Israelites.

- In the Old Testament, food symbolizes God's provision and blessings. The manna provided to the Israelites in the wilderness (Exodus 16:4) represents God's care and sustenance. Sharing a meal was also central to the covenant relationship between God and His people, symbolizing fellowship and communion.
- The New Testament continues this theme, with Jesus using food in many of His teachings and miracles. His first miracle was creating wine from water. The Last Supper, where Jesus broke bread and shared wine with His disciples, is one of the most significant spiritual events in the Christian tradition, symbolizing His body and blood given for the salvation of humanity (Matthew 26:26-28).

Food also plays a crucial role in other spiritual traditions. In Hinduism, the concept of *prasad* involves offering food to the deities, which is then consumed as a blessed sacrament by the devotees. In Buddhism, mindfulness extends to eating, with practices encouraging being fully present and grateful for each bite.

## SCRIPTURAL INSIGHTS

The Bible offers numerous insights into the significance of diet in spiritual life. Here are a few key passages:

- **Genesis 1:29 (NIV):** "Then God said, 'I give you every seed-bearing plant on the face of the whole earth and every tree that has fruit with seed in it. They will be yours for food.'" This passage highlights the provision of plant-based foods as a divine gift.

- **Proverbs 25:27 (NIV):** "It is not good to eat too much honey, nor is it honorable to search out matters that are too deep." This proverb warns against overindulgence, advocating for moderation and balance.
- **1 Corinthians 10:31 (NIV):** "So whether you eat or drink or whatever you do, do it all for the glory of God." This verse encourages believers to honor God in all aspects of life, including their dietary choices.
- **Matthew 6:11 (NIV):** "Give us today our daily bread." In the Lord's Prayer, Jesus teaches us to rely on God for our daily sustenance, recognizing food as a provision from the divine, as manna was for the Israelites.

## CASE STUDY: MICHAEL'S DISCOVERY

Michael, a busy professional and devout Christian, often found himself eating on the run, choosing convenience foods that were quick but not necessarily nourishing. Over time, he noticed a decline in energy levels and a growing sense of disconnection from his spiritual practices.

Inspired by a sermon on the importance of treating the body as a temple of the Holy Spirit, Michael decided to change. He began by incorporating more whole foods into his diet, focusing on fruits, vegetables, lean proteins, and whole grains. He also started saying grace before meals, expressing gratitude for the food and its source.

As Michael embraced these changes, he noticed significant improvements in his physical health. He had more energy and better digestion and even lost a few pounds. More importantly, he felt a renewed connection to his faith —expressing gratitude transformed mealtime into a spiritual practice, deepening his relationship with God.

## SPIRITUAL INSIGHTS FROM DIETARY CHANGES

Michael's journey illustrates how dietary changes impact spiritual well-being. Here are some spiritual insights that can be gained from nourishing both body and soul:

**1. Connection to the Divine:** Mindful eating and gratitude practices can enhance your connection to the divine, turning everyday activities into opportunities for worship.

**2. Embodiment of Faith:** Making intentional food choices can express your faith, reflecting your commitment to honoring the body as a temple of the Holy Spirit.

**3. Awareness and Presence:** Mindful eating fosters awareness and presence, helping you stay grounded in the moment and more attuned to your body's needs.

**4. Gratitude and Abundance:** Practicing gratitude for your food can cultivate a sense of abundance and appreciation for the blessings in your life, enhancing your overall well-being.

**5. Holistic Health:** Recognizing the interconnectedness of physical and spiritual health can inspire you to make choices that support both, leading to a more balanced and fulfilling life.

# AFTERWORD

Food is more than just fuel for the body; it is a powerful tool for nurturing the soul. Making intentional food choices can nourish your body and spirit, foster a deeper connection to the divine, and enhance your overall well-being.

Recognize the sacredness of food, and let your choices reflect your reverence for your body as a temple of your spirit. By embodying these principles, you can uncover the profound influence of diet on your spiritual path.

# CHAPTER 7

# INTEGRATING MEDITATION WITH DIET AND EXERCISE

Meditation can enhance physical and spiritual well-being with mindful eating and a nutritious diet. This chapter explores the benefits of meditation, techniques for integrating meditation with diet, personal stories and testimonials, and practical tips for creating a holistic routine that incorporates both practices.

## MEDITATION AND ITS BENEFITS

Meditation is a practice that involves focusing the mind on a particular object, thought, or activity to achieve a mentally clear and emotionally calm state. In its simplest form, it involves sitting with eyes closed, noticing the thoughts that come into the mind, and releasing them as soon as they appear. It has been practiced for centuries across various cultures and spiritual traditions. The benefits of meditation are well-documented and include:

**1. Stress Reduction:** Meditation is known for reducing stress by promoting relaxation and lowering cortisol levels, the hormone associated with stress (Goyal et al., 2014).

**2. Improved Focus and Concentration:** Regular meditation can enhance attention span and cognitive function, making it easier to focus on tasks and remain present.

**3. Emotional Health:** Meditation can improve emotional well-being by increasing self-awareness and promoting a positive outlook. It has been shown to reduce symptoms of depression and anxiety.

**4. Spiritual Connection:** Meditation provides a pathway to deeper spiritual awareness and connection, providing a space for reflection, prayer, and communion with the divine.

It would be best if you meditated regularly to gain the most profound results, but many find it excruciatingly difficult to break out of the trance of everyday life. Even five minutes of meditation can have positive effects. If you do not meditate regularly now, try to find five minutes each day to take a deep breath, close your eyes, and dismiss any thoughts that come into your mind. Just listen to the world around you and for the still, small voice of the Holy Spirit. Try to make meditation a regular part of your day.

## COMBINING DIET WITH MEDITATION

Here are some techniques for integrating meditation with your dietary habits:

**1. Pre-Meal Meditation:** Taking a few minutes to meditate before meals can help you transition from the busyness of the day to a state of mindfulness. This practice can enhance your awareness and appreciation of the food you are about to eat.

**2. Mindful Eating Meditation:** Practice being fully

present with each bite during meals. Focus on the flavors, textures, and aromas of the food. This mindfulness can help you savor each bite and develop a deeper connection to the nourishment you receive.

**3. Post-Meal Reflection:** After eating, take a moment to reflect on the experience. Consider how the food made you feel physically and emotionally. This reflection can enhance your awareness of the impact of your dietary choices on your well-being.

**4. Gratitude Meditation:** Incorporate gratitude into your meditation practice by expressing thanks for the food and the hands that prepared it. This practice can foster a sense of appreciation and connection to the source of your nourishment.

**5. 80 Percent Rule:** Stop eating before you are full, at about 80 percent full. The body is programmed to take advantage of food and consume more than is needed for healthy body weight and fitness.

## PERSONAL STORIES AND TESTIMONIALS

Personal stories can illustrate the power of integrating meditation with diet. Let's explore the journey of Lisa, who experienced significant changes in her well-being through these practices.

**CASE STUDY: Lisa's Experience**

Lisa, a school teacher and mother of two, often felt overwhelmed by her busy schedule. She struggled with stress and found herself turning to unhealthy comfort foods for relief. Realizing the toll this was taking on her physical and emotional health, Lisa decided to change.

She began by incorporating a simple meditation practice into her daily routine. Each morning, she spent ten minutes in quiet reflection, focusing on her breath and setting intentions for the day. She also started eating more slowly, paying attention to her hunger and fullness cues, and savoring each bite of her meals. Her children picked up on her changed attitude and behaved better at the table.

Lisa noticed immediate benefits from her meditation practice. She felt more centered and less reactive to stress. Over time, her relationship with food also improved. By eating mindfully, she could enjoy her meals more fully and make healthier food choices. She drastically reduced her consumption of carbohydrates. Her newfound gratitude and connection to her food enhanced her overall well-being.

Lisa's journey shows how integrating meditation with diet can transform physical and spiritual health. She found greater peace, balance, and fulfillment by creating a holistic routine incorporating these practices.

## INTEGRATING MEDITATION AND EXERCISE

Just as with eating, taking a mindful approach to exercise can enhance the benefits of exercise. Here are the key benefits with examples:

- **Enhanced Mental Clarity and Focus:** Practicing mindfulness meditation before or after a workout can improve concentration during exercise and enhance overall mental clarity throughout the day.
- **Reduced Stress and Anxiety:** Combining yoga (which integrates physical postures with

meditation) helps lower cortisol levels, leading to reduced stress and anxiety.

- **Improved Emotional Well-being:** Meditative practices like tai chi, incorporating slow, deliberate movements with focused breathing, can improve mood and emotional stability. Even a walk can become a meditation.
- **Better Physical Performance and Recovery:** Incorporating mindfulness techniques during strength training can improve muscle engagement and form. At the same time, post-workout meditation can aid in faster recovery by promoting relaxation and reducing muscle tension.
- **Increased Mind-Body Awareness:** Pilates, which emphasizes controlled movements and breathing, enhances body awareness and mindfulness, leading to better posture and coordination.
- **Enhanced Flexibility and Balance:** Doing a practice like qigong, which combines gentle physical exercises with breath control and meditation, can improve flexibility, balance, and overall physical coordination.
- **Boosted Immune System:** Regularly practicing meditative exercises like mindful walking or yoga can reduce inflammation and strengthen the immune system by lowering stress hormones and promoting a state of calm.
- **Better Sleep Quality:** A gentle stretching routine combined with deep breathing exercises before bedtime can help relax the body and mind, improving sleep quality.

- **Increased Motivation and Consistency:** Setting a positive intention through a brief meditation session before exercising can increase motivation and help maintain a consistent workout routine.
- **Holistic Health Improvement:** Integrating meditation with cardiovascular exercises like running or cycling can improve mental health (through stress reduction) and physical health (through cardiovascular benefits).

THESE COMBINED practices promote physical fitness and foster mental resilience and emotional balance, contributing to a comprehensive approach to overall well-being.

# AFTERWORD

Integrating meditation with diet and exercise offers a holistic approach to well-being that nourishes both the body and soul. Eating more slowly, expressing gratitude, and incorporating meditation into your daily routine can enhance your physical health and deepen your spiritual connection.

When you adopt a mindful approach to your exercise routine, you're not just working out but connecting your body with the divine. This shift in perspective can lead to a more holistic approach to your well-being, allowing you to discover meditation and diet's profound impact on your life.

# MAKE A DIFFERENCE

MAKE A DIFFERENCE WITH YOUR REVIEW

**Unlock the Power of Generosity**

"Giving is not just about making a donation. It's about making a difference." - Kathy Calvin

People who give without expecting anything in return often find more joy and fulfillment in life. So, if we can do that together, let's make it happen.

To make this a reality, I have a simple question for you...

Would you help someone you've never met, even if you never got credit for it?

Who is this person you ask? They are just like you. Or, at least, like you used to be. They seek balance, want to make a difference, and seek guidance but are unsure where to start.

Our mission is to make the harmony of body, mind, and spirit accessible to everyone. Everything we do stems from that mission, and the only way for us to accomplish that mission is by reaching... everyone.

This is where you come in. Most people judge a book by its cover (and its reviews). So here's my ask on behalf of a seeking spirit you've never met:

Please help that questing spirit by leaving this book a review.

Your gift costs no money and takes less than 60 seconds to make real, but it can change a fellow spirit's life forever. Your review could help...

- ...one more person discover the joy of holistic wellness.
- ...one more reader find the balance they've been searching for.
- ...one more soul connect with their inner wisdom.
- ...one more individual transform their life.

To get that 'feel good' feeling and help this person for real, you only have to leave a review, which takes less than 60 seconds.

Click the link below to leave your review:

Click here to leave a review. Or point your phone at the QR code.

If you feel good about helping a faceless spirit, you are my kind of person. Welcome to the club. You're one of us.

I'm even more excited to help you achieve harmony faster and easier than you imagine. You'll love the insights and strategies I share in the coming chapters.

Thank you from the bottom of my heart. Now, back to our regularly scheduled programming.

- Your biggest fan, Elliott Middleton

PS - Fun fact: If you provide something of value to another person, it makes you more valuable to them. If you believe this book will help someone you know, send it their way.

# CHAPTER 8

# FASTING FOR SPIRITUAL WELL-BEING

Of all the lifestyle changes I have made in my quest for body-mind-spirit integration, fasting has had the greatest impact. Fasting has enabled leaps and bounds of spiritual advancement.

Fasting is deeply rooted in many religious traditions and is known for its physical benefits and spiritual significance. While fasting is often associated with deprivation, it is a tool for spiritual growth, self-discipline, and heightened awareness. This chapter describes the historical and religious perspectives on fasting, its health and spiritual benefits, practical tips for fasting, and inspiring case studies of individuals who have embraced this practice.

## HISTORICAL AND RELIGIOUS PERSPECTIVES ON FASTING

Fasting has been practiced for millennia across different cultures and religions for purification, penance, and spiritual discipline.

- **Christianity:** The Bible is filled with references to fasting. Jesus Himself fasted for forty days and forty nights in the wilderness before beginning His public ministry (Matthew 4:2). The early Christians continued this practice, enhancing their spiritual focus and devotion. Lent, a season of fasting and repentance, commemorates Jesus' forty-day fast and is observed by many Christian denominations.
- **Islam:** Fasting is one of the Five Pillars of Faith in Islam. During the holy month of Ramadan, Muslims fast from dawn until sunset, refraining from food, drink, and other physical needs. This practice is seen as a way to purify the soul, practice self-discipline, and empathize with the less fortunate.
- **Judaism:** Fasting is integral to Jewish religious practice, particularly on Yom Kippur, the Day of Atonement. This holiest day in the Jewish calendar involves a 25-hour fast that reflects repentance, humility, and spiritual renewal. Moses fasted for 40 days on Mount Sinai (Exodus 34:28).
- **Buddhism:** Many Buddhists practice intermittent fasting as part of their spiritual discipline, abstaining from food after noon to enhance their meditation and mindfulness practices.

## HEALTH BENEFITS OF FASTING

Modern science has begun to uncover the physical benefits

of fasting, supporting what ancient traditions have long espoused. Here are some key health benefits:

**1. Improved Metabolic Health:** Fasting can improve insulin sensitivity, lower blood sugar levels, and reduce inflammation, promoting better metabolic health. Research from Johns Hopkins Medicine highlights that intermittent fasting can promote fat loss while preserving muscle mass, enhance heart health by lowering blood pressure and resting heart rates, and support cognitive function. Additionally, studies suggest that intermittent fasting may help prevent obesity and type 2 diabetes by reducing insulin resistance and lowering levels of fasting glucose and insulin (Johns Hopkins Medicine, 2024).

**2. Enhanced Brain Function:** Fasting has been shown to support brain health by promoting the production of brain-derived neurotrophic factor (BDNF), which protects brain cells and enhances cognitive function.

**3. Cellular Repair and Autophagy:** During fasting, the body initiates cellular repair processes and autophagy, where cells remove damaged components and regenerate. This can help protect against diseases like cancer and neurodegenerative disorders.

**4. Weight Management:** Fasting can support weight management by reducing overall calorie intake and promoting weight loss, especially with a healthy diet.

**5. Longevity:** Some studies suggest that intermittent fasting can extend lifespan by improving metabolic health and reducing the risk of chronic diseases.

**6. Fasting and the Immune System:** Scientific research finds that a three-day fast can rejuvenate the immune system to its peak performance. A study at the University of Southern California revealed that fasting for 72 hours can notably enhance immune system function.

The process involves the body breaking down and regenerating immune cells, particularly old or damaged ones, thereby increasing the number of new, healthy immune cells (Leonard Davis School of Gerontology, 2018).

## SPIRITUAL BENEFITS OF FASTING

Beyond the physical benefits, fasting offers profound spiritual rewards. Here are some ways fasting can enhance spiritual well-being:

**1. Increased Spiritual Awareness:** Fasting helps quiet the mind and body, making connecting with the divine easier and deepening your spiritual practice. It creates a space for reflection, prayer, and meditation, allowing for heightened spiritual awareness. Spiritual senses are sharpened.

**2. Self-Discipline and Control:** Fasting cultivates self-discipline and control over physical desires, fostering a sense of mastery over the body and mind. This discipline can extend to other areas of life, enhancing overall self-control and focus. I call this "showing the body who's boss."

**3. Repentance and Humility:** Fasting is often associated with repentance and humility. It is a way to acknowledge our weaknesses, seek forgiveness, and commit to spiritual growth and renewal.

**4. Empathy and Compassion:** Fasting can foster empathy and compassion for those who regularly experience hunger and deprivation. It encourages solidarity with the less fortunate and inspires acts of charity and service.

**5. Spiritual Renewal:** Many people find that fasting leads to spiritual renewal and revitalization. It is a time to reconnect with core values, deepen faith, and seek divine guidance.

## PRACTICAL TIPS FOR FASTING

Here are some practical tips to help you incorporate fasting into your spiritual practice:

**1. Start Slowly:** If you are new to fasting, start with shorter fasts and gradually increase the duration as your body adapts. Begin with intermittent fasting, abstaining from food for 12-16 hours, and eating during the remaining hours.

**2. Stay Hydrated:** Drink plenty of water during your fasting period. Herbal teas and clear broths can also help maintain hydration and provide nutrients.

**3. Choose the Right Time:** Plan your fast when you can focus on spiritual practices without significant distractions. Weekends or spiritual retreats are ideal for extended fasts. Once you become adept at fasting, you will be able to do it at any time.

**4. Listen to Your Body:** Listen to your body's signals and adjust your fasting routine accordingly. If you feel lightheaded, weak, or unwell, consider shortening the fast or modifying your approach.

**5. Incorporate Prayer and Meditation:** Use the time you eat to engage in prayer, meditation, or other spiritual activities. This helps maintain focus and enhances the spiritual benefits of fasting.

**6. Break the Fast Mindfully:** When ending your fast, do so gradually with light, nutritious foods. Avoid overeating or consuming heavy, rich foods immediately after fasting. Bone broth contains lots of protein and is easy to digest, making it an excellent choice for breaking a longer fast.

## CASE STUDY: JACK'S SPIRITUAL RENEWAL

Jack, a busy marketing executive, had always struggled to find time for spiritual practices amidst his hectic schedule. He decided to try fasting to deepen his spiritual life and gain clarity on important decisions. Jack began with a 24-hour dinner-to-dinner fast once a week, dedicating the day to prayer, meditation, and reflection.

The first few fasts were challenging, but Jack soon noticed himself changing. He felt more focused and spiritually attuned, gaining insights and perspectives that had eluded him before. The discipline of fasting also helped Jack develop better self-control in other areas of his life, improving his work-life balance and personal relationships.

As he continued his fasting practice, Jack experienced a deep sense of spiritual renewal. He felt more connected to his faith and aligned with his life's purpose. Fasting transformed his approach to spirituality, providing a powerful tool for growth and self-discovery.

## SPIRITUAL INSIGHTS FROM FASTING

Fasting offers a wealth of spiritual insights that can enhance your journey of faith and self-awareness:

**1. Trust in Divine Provision:** Fasting reinforces the belief that a higher power meets our needs. It is an act of surrender, trusting that the divine will provide for our physical and spiritual nourishment.

**2. Clarity and Insight:** The mental clarity and focus gained through fasting can lead to spiritual insights and revelations. It is a time to seek guidance, reflect on life's purpose, and make crucial decisions.

**3. Detachment and Simplicity:** Fasting encourages detachment from material comforts and fosters a sense of simplicity. This detachment can enhance spiritual growth by allowing one to focus on what truly matters.

**4. Gratitude and Appreciation:** The experience of abstaining from food fosters gratitude for the blessings we often take for granted. It deepens our appreciation for the nourishment we receive and the abundance in our lives.

**5. Spiritual Strength and Resilience:** Fasting builds spiritual and physical strength and resilience, helping us face life's challenges with greater faith and determination. It also strengthens our commitment to our spiritual path.

I have found fasting to be the most essential element of my new lifestyle, and I am committed to body, mind, and spirit unity. My preferred fast is a 36-hour water-only fast, which I incorporate into my routine several times a month. For instance, I might fast from dinner on a Sunday night to breakfast on Tuesday morning. On the fasting day in between, I experience a remarkable boost in mental clarity, focus, and productivity.

Once every few months, I fast for three to five days to let my immune system reset to optimal condition. As mentioned, a three-day water fast is optimal for this.

# AFTERWORD

Fasting is a spiritual practice that offers numerous physical and spiritual benefits. By integrating fasting into your routine, you can enhance your spiritual well-being, develop greater self-discipline, and gain profound insights into your life and faith, all of which can lead to personal growth and self-discovery.

Embrace this ancient practice with an open heart and discover its impact on your spiritual journey. Whether seeking clarity, renewal, or a deeper connection with the divine, fasting provides a pathway to spiritual growth and self-discovery.

# CHAPTER 9

# THE POWER OF COMMUNITY

Human beings are inherently social creatures. We thrive on connection, support, and shared experiences. This chapter explores the importance of community in maintaining dietary and spiritual practices, offers practical tips for building a supportive environment, and highlights inspiring success stories of individuals who have found strength and resilience through community support.

## IMPORTANCE OF COMMUNITY SUPPORT

Being part of a supportive group can provide numerous benefits, including:

**1. Emotional Support:** A strong community offers a network of people who can provide empathy, understanding, and encouragement during difficult times. This emotional support can be invaluable in maintaining mental health and resilience.

**2. Accountability:** Being part of a community can help you stay accountable for your goals. Whether you stick to a healthy diet, exercise regularly, or maintain spiritual practices, having others to share your journey with can motivate and commit you.

**3. Shared Knowledge and Resources:** Communities are a rich source of shared knowledge and resources. Members can exchange tips, recipes, and advice, enhancing everyone's ability to make informed and healthy choices.

**4. Spiritual Growth:** Community engagement can deepen your spiritual practice. Shared worship, prayer, and meditation can enhance your connection to the divine and provide a sense of belonging and purpose.

**5. Social Connection:** Loneliness and social isolation can harm mental and physical health. Being part of a community fosters social connections, reducing loneliness and enhancing overall well-being.

Finding a supportive community in the United States can be difficult, but it is necessary to advance along the path of body-mind-spirit unification. Community support is required in a church, synagogue, mosque, or simply a group of like-minded people.

## BIBLICAL EXAMPLES OF COMMUNITY SUPPORT

The Bible provides numerous examples of the importance of community support. In the early Christian church, community was central to the believers' lives:

- **Acts 2:42 (NIV):** "They devoted themselves to the apostles' teaching and fellowship, to the breaking of bread and prayer." The early Christians were committed to community, sharing meals, and supporting one another in their spiritual journeys.

- **Galatians 6:2 (NIV):** "Carry each other's burdens, and in this way, you will fulfill the law of Christ." This verse underscores the importance of supporting one another and sharing the load during challenging times.
- **Hebrews 10:24-25 (NIV):** "And let us consider how we may spur one another on toward love and good deeds, not giving up meeting together, as some are in the habit of doing, but encouraging one another—and all the more as you see the Day approaching." These verses emphasize the importance of gathering together for mutual encouragement and support, especially during the last days.

## CREATING A SUPPORTIVE ENVIRONMENT

Building or joining a supportive community can significantly enhance your ability to maintain healthy dietary and spiritual practices. Here are some practical tips for creating a supportive environment:

**1. Identify Your Needs:** Consider what type of support you need. Are you seeking a community focused on healthy eating, spiritual growth, or both? Identifying your needs can help you find or create a group that aligns with your goals.

**2. Seek Like-Minded Individuals:** Look for individuals or groups that share your values and goals. This could be through local religious organizations, community centers, or online forums.

**3. Be Active and Engaged:** Participation is critical to building a supportive community. Attend meetings, engage in discussions, and offer support to others. The more you put into the community, the more you will get out of it.

**4. Organize Regular Activities:** Plan regular activities that align with your goals. This could include potluck dinners with healthy recipes, group meditation sessions, or book clubs focused on spiritual growth.

**5. Share and Learn:** Encourage the exchange of knowledge and resources within the community. Share your experiences, recipes, and tips, and be open to learning from others.

**6. Provide Mutual Support:** Offer emotional support and encouragement to fellow members. Celebrate each other's successes and comfort each other during challenging times.

## SUCCESS STORIES

Let's explore some inspiring success stories of individuals who have found strength and resilience through community support.

**CASE STUDY: Mary's Journey of Finding Community Support through Her Church**

Mary, a single mother of two, struggled with maintaining a healthy lifestyle amidst her busy schedule running a retail outlet. She often felt overwhelmed and isolated. She sought support and joined a health and wellness group at her local church. The group met weekly to discuss healthy eating, share recipes, and support each other in their spiritual journeys.

The community gave Mary the encouragement and accountability she needed to make positive changes. She started cooking healthier meals, participating in group workouts, and practicing regular prayer and meditation. The emotional support from the group helped her stay motivated and committed to her goals.

Mary found a renewed sense of purpose and well-being through the group's shared knowledge and mutual encouragement.

## PRACTICAL TIPS FOR BUILDING COMMUNITY

**1. Start or Join a Group:** If you can't find a suitable community, consider starting your own. Invite friends, family, or like-minded individuals to join you in your journey toward better health and spiritual growth.

**2. Use Technology:** Leverage technology to connect with others. Online forums, social media groups, and virtual meetups can provide valuable support and resources, especially if in-person gatherings are not feasible.

**3. Set Common Goals:** Establish common goals and objectives for the community. These could relate to healthy eating, exercise, or spiritual practices. Having shared goals can enhance accountability and motivation.

**4. Encourage Inclusivity:** Create an inclusive and welcoming environment where everyone feels valued and supported. Encourage open communication and respect for diverse perspectives and experiences.

**5. Celebrate Successes:** Celebrate the achievements and milestones of community members. Recognizing and celebrating successes can foster a positive and supportive atmosphere.

## SPIRITUAL INSIGHTS FROM COMMUNITY SUPPORT

Community engagement can provide spiritual insights and enhance your overall well-being. Here are some spiritual insights that can be gained from community support:

**1. Unity and Connection:** Being part of a community fosters a sense of unity and connection with others. It reminds us that we are part of a larger, interconnected whole, not alone on our journey.

**2. Encouragement and Growth:** Community support provides encouragement and inspiration, helping us grow and develop spiritually and personally. It offers a space for shared learning and mutual support.

**3. Service and Compassion:** Engaging with a community encourages acts of service and compassion. It provides opportunities to support and uplift others, reflecting the teachings of love and kindness in many spiritual traditions.

**4. Strength and Resilience:** Community support can enhance our strength and resilience, helping us navigate challenges with greater confidence and grace. It provides a network of support that can help us overcome obstacles and achieve our goals.

I have a "fasting buddy" who has also embraced the 36-hour water-only fast. We coordinate our fasts. Knowing I am not fasting alone is tremendously supportive when we commit to a fast.

# AFTERWORD

Experience the transformative power of community. Joining a supportive group can significantly boost your physical, mental, and spiritual well-being. By aligning with a community that mirrors your values and aspirations, you open the door to a wealth of support, motivation, and responsibility, crucial for maintaining a healthy lifestyle and spiritual practices.

Embrace the opportunity to connect with others, share your journey, and discover the impact of community on your life.

# CHAPTER 10

# CULTURAL AND TRADITIONAL INFLUENCES

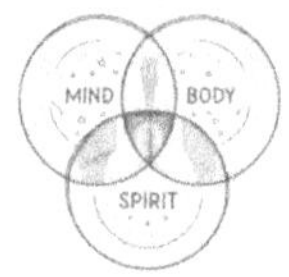

istorically, a community's dietary habits were deeply influenced by cultural and traditional practices passed down through generations. These practices reflected the community's culinary heritage and embodied its spiritual beliefs and values. Few follow traditional dietary practices today, but all can learn from the most successful ones.

This chapter will discuss the significance of traditional diets, their spiritual meaning, and how modern nutrition can benefit from incorporating these practices. Additionally, we will examine inspiring case studies of traditional diets and their impact on health and spirituality.

## CULTURAL DIETARY PRACTICES

Different cultures have unique dietary practices often rooted in their historical, geographical, and spiritual contexts. These traditional diets are about food, community, ritual, and connection to the natural world.

· · ·

**MEDITERRANEAN DIET:** Known for its emphasis on fresh fruits, vegetables, whole grains, nuts, and olive oil, the Mediterranean diet also includes moderate consumption of fish and poultry. This diet is associated with reduced risks of heart disease and other chronic illnesses. The Mediterranean lifestyle promotes healthy eating, social interactions, and physical activity, reflecting a holistic approach to well-being (Trichopoulou et al., 2014).

**OKINAWAN DIET:** The traditional diet of Okinawa, Japan, is rich in vegetables, tofu, sweet potatoes, and seafood. Okinawans practice "Hara Hachi Bu," which means eating until 80 percent full. Combined with their nutrient-dense diet, this practice is believed to contribute to their longevity and low rates of chronic diseases (Willcox et al., 2009).

**INDIAN AYURVEDIC DIET:** Ayurveda, the ancient Indian system of medicine, emphasizes a balanced diet tailored to an individual's *dosha* (body type). It promotes eating fresh, seasonal, locally sourced foods and incorporating spices like turmeric, ginger, and cumin, which have medicinal properties. The Ayurvedic diet is about physical health and maintaining balance and harmony within the body and mind (Lad, 1984).

## RELIGIOUS DIETARY LAWS

Many religious traditions have dietary laws that reflect their spiritual values and beliefs. These practices often emphasize purity, self-discipline, and respect for the sanctity of food.

- **Kosher Diet:** In Judaism, kosher dietary laws dictate the types of foods that can be eaten and how they must be prepared. These laws are rooted in the Torah and emphasize cleanliness, ethical treatment of animals, and the spiritual significance of food (Deuteronomy 14:3-21).
- **Halal Diet:** In Islam, halal dietary laws govern what is permissible. Foods must be prepared according to Islamic guidelines, which include ethical animal slaughter and avoidance of certain prohibited items like pork and alcohol. These practices ensure purity and adherence to Islamic principles (Quran 5:3).
- **Christian Fasting Practices:** Many Christian denominations observe fasting periods, such as Lent, which involves abstaining from certain foods to practice self-discipline and spiritual reflection. Fasting is a way to draw closer to God and seek spiritual renewal (Matthew 6:16-18). There are no dietary restrictions in Christianity.

## CASE STUDIES OF TRADITIONAL DIETS

Let's explore some case studies of traditional diets and their impact on health and spirituality.

CASE STUDY: **The Mediterranean Lifestyle**

Maria, a Greek woman in her 70s, has always followed the Mediterranean diet, a tradition from her grandmother. Her diet includes fresh vegetables, fruits, whole grains, olive oil, and moderate fish and poultry. Meals are often shared with family and friends, fostering a sense of community and belonging.

Maria's lifestyle reflects the holistic approach of the Mediterranean diet. She enjoys good health and a rich social life. Her spiritual practices include gratitude for the food she eats and regular participation in community events. Maria's story illustrates how healthy traditional diets can support physical health and enhance social and spiritual well-being.

**Case Study: The Okinawan Longevity**

Hiroshi, an 85-year-old Okinawan, attributes his long life to the traditional Okinawan diet and lifestyle. He eats a diet rich in vegetables, tofu, sweet potatoes, and seafood. Hiroshi practices "Hara Hachi Bu," eating until he is 80 percent full, which helps maintain his weight and overall health.

Hiroshi's daily routine includes physical activity, social interactions, and spiritual practices such as meditation and prayer. The Okinawan diet, combined with these holistic practices, has contributed to his longevity and vitality. Hiroshi's experience also highlights the benefits of healthy traditional diets and their role in promoting long-term health and spiritual well-being.

## INTEGRATING CULTURAL PRACTICES WITH MODERN NUTRITION

Modern nutrition can benefit significantly from incorporating healthy traditional dietary practices. Here are some tips for integrating these practices into your diet:

**1. Embrace Whole Foods:** Traditional diets emphasize whole, unprocessed foods. Add more fresh fruits, vegetables, whole grains, nuts, and lean proteins to your meals.

**2. Practice Moderation:** Many traditional diets include moderation practices, such as "Hara Hachi Bu" in Okinawa. Avoid overeating by listening to your body's hunger and fullness cues.

**3. Use Healing Spices:** Incorporate spices with medicinal properties into your cooking. Turmeric, ginger, garlic, and cumin are staples in many traditional diets and offer numerous health benefits.

**4. Prioritize Community and Rituals:** Traditional diets often include communal meals and rituals. Make mealtime a social and spiritual experience by sharing meals with family and friends and practicing gratitude.

**5. Respect for Nature:** Traditional diets emphasize a connection to nature and seasonal eating. Choose locally sourced, seasonal foods to align with these principles and support sustainable practices.

## PRACTICAL TIPS FOR INTEGRATING CULTURAL PRACTICES

We can benefit from traditional diets even if they don't originate in our ancestral culture. We can:

**1. Explore New Cuisines:** Experiment with recipes from different cultural traditions. This can introduce you to new flavors and healthful ingredients.

**2. Learn from Elders:** Seek knowledge from older generations who practice successful traditional diets. Their wisdom and experience can provide valuable insights into healthy eating.

**3. Incorporate Spiritual Practices:** Integrate spiritual practices from traditional diets, such as saying grace before meals, to enhance your connection to food and spirituality.

**4. Create a Balanced Plate:** Follow the principles of traditional diets by creating balanced meals that include a variety of food groups. Aim for a colorful plate with vegetables, proteins, and whole grains.

**5. Stay Physically Active:** Many traditional lifestyles include physical activity as a natural part of daily life. Incorporate regular exercise into your routine to complement your dietary habits. Take the stairs.

## SPIRITUAL INSIGHTS FROM CULTURAL PRACTICES

Embracing traditional dietary practices can provide spiritual insights and enhance your overall well-being. Here are some spiritual insights that can be gained from these practices:

**1. Connection to Ancestry:** Traditional diets can connect us to our ancestors and cultural heritage. They remind us of the wisdom passed down through generations and the importance of preserving these traditions.

**2. Respect for Creation:** Traditional diets often emphasize respect for nature and the environment. This respect can deepen our connection to the natural world and foster a sense of stewardship.

**3. Gratitude and Mindfulness:** Saying grace encourages gratitude and mindfulness. These practices can transform mealtime into a spiritual experience and enhance our appreciation for the nourishment we receive.

**4. Community and Belonging:** Traditional diets often involve communal meals and rituals, fostering a sense of community and belonging. These social connections are essential for spiritual well-being and personal growth.

**5. Balance and Harmony:** Traditional diets promote balance and harmony in our eating habits and lifestyle. This holistic approach can enhance our overall health and spiritual well-being.

# AFTERWORD

Successful cultural and traditional dietary practices offer valuable insights into healthy eating and spiritual well-being. By embracing these practices, we can enhance our physical health, deepen our spiritual connection, and foster a sense of community and belonging. Maria and Hiroshi's stories illustrate the impact of some traditional diets on health and spirituality.

We can unlock their supercharging spiritual power by embracing the wisdom of cultural dietary practices and integrating them into our modern lifestyles. Whether it's through exploring new cuisines, practicing gratitude, or reconnecting with our cultural heritage—or a different one —traditional diets offer a clear pathway to holistic health and spiritual fulfillment.

# CHAPTER 11

# THE SCIENCE OF GRATITUDE AND WELL-BEING

Expressing gratitude to God for our gifts is more than just an emotion; it is a practice that can transform our mental, physical, and spiritual well-being.

Scientific research has increasingly supported the idea that expressing gratitude affects health, fostering a more positive outlook and enhancing our overall quality of life. This chapter covers the science behind the benefits of expressing gratitude (or "gratitude," as it is commonly called), its psychological benefits, and practical ways to incorporate gratitude into daily life, particularly in the context of food and nourishment.

## PSYCHOLOGICAL BENEFITS OF EXPRESSING GRATITUDE

Gratitude has been extensively studied within the fields of psychology and neuroscience, revealing a multitude of benefits. Here are some of the key findings:

**1. Enhanced Mental Health:** Research consistently shows that practicing gratitude can reduce symptoms of depression and anxiety. Gratitude shifts focus away from negative emotions and thoughts, fostering a more positive outlook (Emmons & McCullough, 2003).

**2. Improved Sleep Quality:** Studies have found that individuals who regularly practice gratitude experience better sleep quality. Reflecting on positive experiences before bed can create a peaceful mind conducive to restful sleep (Wood et al., 2009).

**3. Increased Emotional Resilience:** Gratitude can bolster emotional resilience, helping individuals cope more effectively with stress and adversity. It enhances a sense of connectedness and support, which is crucial during challenging times (Southwick & Charney, 2012).

**4. Stronger Relationships:** Expressing gratitude strengthens relationships by fostering feelings of appreciation and mutual respect. It encourages positive interactions and enhances social bonds (Algoe, Haidt, & Gable, 2008).

**5. Greater Life Satisfaction:** Regular gratitude practice is linked to overall life satisfaction. By focusing on what one has rather than what one lacks, gratitude promotes a sense of contentment and well-being (Wood, Froh, & Geraghty, 2010).

## GRATITUDE PRACTICES RELATED TO FOOD

Incorporating gratitude into our relationship with food can enhance physical and spiritual well-being. Here are some gratitude practices related to food:

**1. Saying Grace:** Saying grace before meals is a traditional practice that fosters gratitude. Giving thanks to the food, the people who prepared it, and its divine provision can transform mealtime into a spiritual experience.

**2. Mindful Eating:** Practicing mindful eating involves

being fully present during meals, savoring each bite, and appreciating the flavors, textures, and aromas. This mindfulness can enhance your enjoyment and foster a sense of gratitude for the nourishment provided.

**3. Reflecting on the Journey of Food:** Consider your food's journey to reach your plate. Reflecting on the farmers who grew the produce, the workers who harvested it, and the cooks who prepared it can deepen your appreciation for the nourishment you receive.

**4. Keeping a Gratitude Journal:** Maintain a gratitude journal where you write down things you are grateful for daily, including your meals. Reflecting on the food you eat and the nourishment it provides can reinforce a sense of gratitude and appreciation.

## PERSONAL STORIES AND REFLECTIONS

Personal stories can illustrate the power of gratitude. Let's look at Leah's journey, which saw significant changes in her well-being through gratitude practices related to food.

**CASE STUDY: Leah's Journey of Gratitude**

Leah, a busy educator and mother of three, often rushed through meals and felt disconnected from her food and family. She struggled with stress and felt overwhelmed by her daily responsibilities. A friend suggested that she try practicing gratitude to reconnect and find peace.

Leah started by keeping a gratitude journal, writing down three things she was grateful for daily, including her meals. She also began saying grace before each meal, taking a moment to reflect on the blessings in her life. Over time, Leah noticed significant changes. Her stress levels decreased, she felt more present and connected during meals, and she developed a deeper appreciation for the nourishment her food provided.

Leah's practice of gratitude transformed her relationship with her family. Mealtime became a sacred time for connection and reflection, fostering a sense of unity and togetherness. Emily's journey illustrates gratitude's impact on physical and spiritual well-being.

## SPIRITUAL INSIGHTS FROM GRATITUDE

Practicing gratitude can provide spiritual insights and enhance your overall well-being. Here are some spiritual insights that can be gained from gratitude:

**1. Connection to the Divine:** Expressing gratitude helps us recognize and appreciate the comforting presence of the Holy Spirit in our lives. It fosters a sense of connection and alignment with a higher power.

**2. Awareness and Presence:** Expressing gratitude encourages us to be present and aware of God's blessings. This mindfulness can enhance our spiritual well-being and deepen our appreciation for the present moment.

**3. Humility and Compassion:** Expressing gratitude fosters humility and compassion. It reminds us of the interconnectedness of all life and inspires us to show kindness and appreciation to others.

**4. Abundance and Joy:** Focusing on what we are grateful for cultivates a sense of abundance and joy. It shifts our perspective from scarcity to abundance, enhancing our overall well-being.

# AFTERWORD

"Gratitude" is a practice that can transform your physical, mental, and spiritual well-being. Incorporating gratitude into daily life can enhance your overall sense of joy, connection, and abundance.

Embrace this practice with an open heart and discover its impact on your life. Whether you say grace before a meal, keep a gratitude journal, or take a moment to appreciate the blessings in your life, expressing your gratitude to God can enrich your spiritual journey and foster a deeper connection to the divine.

# CHAPTER 12

# THE ROLE OF PRAYER AND INTENTION

Prayer and focused intention are spiritual tools that can strongly influence our well-being. From ancient religious practices to modern scientific studies, prayer and setting intentions have been shown to foster physical, mental, and spiritual health. More recent scientific research has shown that prayer and focused intention can also affect the physical world.

## POWER OF PRAYER IN HOLISTIC HEALTH

Prayer has been a cornerstone of spiritual practice across cultures and religions. It is a means of communicating with the divine, seeking guidance, and expressing gratitude. The Bible emphasizes the importance of prayer in numerous passages:

- **Philippians 4:6-7 (NIV):** "Do not be anxious about anything, but in every situation, by prayer and petition, with thanksgiving, present your requests to God. And the peace of God, which transcends all understanding, will guard your hearts and your minds in Christ Jesus."

- **James 5:16 (NIV):** "Therefore confess your sins to each other and pray for each other so that you may be healed. The prayer of a righteous person is powerful and effective."

Prayer is a spiritual practice and has tangible benefits for physical health. Research has shown that prayer can reduce stress, lower blood pressure, and improve well-being (Levin, 2011).

An *Adversity and Resilience Science* study discusses the epigenetic consequences of adversity and intervention throughout the lifespan. It highlights that the epigenome displays a remarkable ability to respond to environmental input, including behavioral interventions like diet, exercise, and talk therapies, which include prayer and affirmations (Collins et al., 2020). This is another example of "tuning" one's DNA through epigenetic changes.

When integrated with a mindful diet and exercise, prayer can powerfully enhance the body's ability to heal and maintain health.

## INTENTION AND ITS IMPACT ON PHYSICAL MATTER

Surprising results about human spirituality have emerged in recent years. The concept of intention and its effect on physical matter has been explored in various scientific studies, particularly mind-body medicine. Researchers like Dr. William Tiller and Dr. Claude Swanson and writers like Lynne McTaggart have investigated the power of human consciousness to influence physical reality.

Dr. Tiller's experiments demonstrated that human intention could alter water pH and affect plant growth (Tiller, 2007). Lynne McTaggart's work in *The Intention Experiment* shows how collective intention can lead to measurable changes in physical systems, including healing and material transformation (McTaggart, 2007).

These studies suggest that our thoughts and intentions can impact physical and social environments. The Maharishi International University conducted several studies demonstrating the impact of meditation on reducing violence and crime in cities. One study found that large groups practicing Transcendental Meditation (TM) significantly reduced urban crime rates.

Specifically, the study observed a 28.4% reduction in the murder rate in 206 large U.S. urban areas from 2007 to 2010, when the number of participants in the meditation group exceeded 1,725, which is considered the square root of 1% of the U.S. population at the time (Hagelin, Rainforth, Orme-Johnson, Cavanaugh, Alexander, Shatkin, Davies, Hughes, & Ross, 1999)).

Spiritual power appears to increase exponentially when a group focuses its intention. A critical level seems to occur where the number of meditators exceeds the square root of the number of people comprising one percent of the population. For example, the square root of a population of 1,000,000 is 1,000, the square root of which is 31.62. A group of 32 or more meditators should be able to influence the behavior of a population of one million souls.

## PRACTICAL STEPS FOR INTEGRATING PRAYER AND INTENTION INTO DAILY LIFE

Let's review how incorporating prayer and intention into your daily routine can enhance your spiritual well-being and support a healthy lifestyle. Here are some practical steps to help you get started:

**1. Morning Prayer and Intention Setting:** Begin your day with a morning or intention-setting ritual. Take a few moments to express gratitude, seek guidance, and set positive intentions for the day ahead. In some Eastern traditions, this practice occurs in part while making your bed.

**2. Prayer Before Meals:** Saying grace before meals is a traditional practice that fosters gratitude and mindfulness. Take a moment to thank God for the food, the hands that prepared it, and the nourishment it provides.

**3. Eating with Intention:** Focus on nourishing your body as the temple of your spirit as you eat. Be mindful of your food's flavors, textures, and aromas, and appreciate the nourishment it provides.

**4. Evening Reflection and Prayer:** End your day with reflection and prayer. Review the day's events, express gratitude for the blessings you received, and set intentions for the following day.

**5. Create a Prayer Journal:** Maintain a journal recording your prayers and intentions. Reflect on your experiences and note any changes or insights you observe.

## CASE STUDY: HANNAH'S HEALING JOURNEY

Hannah, a nurse and mother of two, faced a significant health challenge when she was diagnosed with an autoimmune disorder. Conventional treatments provided limited relief, and Hannah sought alternative ways to support her healing process. She began incorporating prayer and intention into her daily routine, setting aside time each morning and evening for reflection and communication with God.

Hannah also started practicing mindful eating, focusing on healing and nourishing her body with each meal. She kept a prayer journal, recording her prayers, intentions, and observations.

Over time, Hannah noticed significant improvements in her health. Her symptoms diminished, and she felt renewed peace and well-being. Hannah's doctors were surprised by her progress, and she attributed her healing to the power of prayer and intention. Her journey highlights these practices' impact on physical and spiritual health.

## SPIRITUAL INSIGHTS FROM PRAYER AND INTENTION

Prayer and intention-setting can provide spiritual insights and enhance your overall well-being. Here are some spiritual insights that can be gained from these practices:

**1. Deepened Faith:** Regular prayer and intention-setting can deepen your faith and strengthen your relationship with the divine. These practices provide a means of seeking guidance, expressing gratitude, and aligning with God's will—the more passionate your prayer, the more powerful it will be.

**2. Mindfulness and Presence:** Prayer and intention encourage mindfulness and presence, helping you stay grounded in the present moment. This awareness can enhance spiritual practices and deepen your connection to the divine.

**3. Healing and Transformation:** The power of prayer

and intention can facilitate healing and transformation physically and spiritually. These practices can help you align with the divine energy of healing and renewal.

**4. Purpose and Direction:** Setting intentions through prayer can provide clarity and direction. It helps you align with your higher purpose and focus on your spiritual goals.

Knowing the power of focused intention, you can formulate prayers that will change the world.

# AFTERWORD

Prayer and intention-setting are powerful spiritual tools that enhance physical, mental, and spiritual well-being. Incorporating these practices into your daily routine can foster a deeper connection to the divine, promote healing and transformation, and enhance your overall sense of peace and fulfillment.

Embrace these practices with an open heart and discover their impact on your life. Whether seeking guidance, healing, or a deeper connection to the divine, prayer and intention-setting provide a pathway to spiritual growth and well-being.

# CHAPTER 13

# INTEGRATING BODY, MIND, AND SPIRIT

Modern science tells us that God "thought up" our complex and amazing Universe (or universes!), which is instantaneously inter-connected in ways that defy the classical laws of physics. The Universe appears conscious in many ways—of our prayers and intentions and demonic forces opposing the light. The Universe contains vibrations of good and evil, and God gives us the choice of which notes and chords we listen to that will resonate within our lives. Affirmations and spiritual texts can tune our DNA to the light. It takes spiritual discernment to recognize God's Word, the language of all creation.

"In the beginning was the Word, and the Word was with God, and the Word was God." —John 1:1

Your life can be a symphony of frequencies that nurture your physical, mental, and spiritual well-being. Combining diet, exercise, and spiritual practices can transform your life into a holistic song of health. This chapter will explore how to design a daily routine that includes diet, exercise, prayer, and meditation. It will also provide practical guidelines for maintaining this balance and share inspiring stories of individuals who have successfully integrated these practices into their daily routines.

## CREATING A HOLISTIC ROUTINE

Designing a daily routine supporting physical and spiritual health requires intentionality and commitment. Here are some steps to help you create a balanced and fulfilling routine:

**1. Start with Intention:** Begin each day setting a clear intention. Take a few moments in the morning to set your goals for the day and connect with your spiritual practice. This could involve a short prayer, meditation, or simply reflecting on your intentions. I say the Lord's Prayer in bed each morning as I wake up, concentrating on each phrase and how it applies to my life.

**2. Plan Balanced Meals:** Incorporate nutritious meals that support your physical health and align with your spiritual values. Focus on whole, unprocessed foods that provide essential nutrients. Consider the spiritual significance of food and the gratitude you feel for its nourishment. Don't eat junk food.

**3. Incorporate Physical Activity:** Physical exercise is essential for overall health. Choose activities you enjoy and provide an opportunity for mindfulness or spiritual reflection, such as yoga, walking, or tai chi. Get some exercise every day.

**4. Give Thanks:** Saying grace and giving thanks for

your food can enhance your appreciation for the nourishment you receive and deepen your spiritual connection.

**5. Schedule Prayer and Meditation:** Dedicate specific times for prayer and meditation during the day. These practices can help you stay grounded, reduce stress, and connect strongly to the divine. If you get thrown off your schedule, find a moment to close your eyes and meditate or pray, even briefly. It is difficult to break out of the daily grind. Even a tiny break helps.

**6. Reflect and Adjust:** Regularly reflect on your routine and adjust as needed. Consider how each aspect of your routine supports your well-being and make changes to enhance balance and harmony.

**7. Incorporate Fasting into Your Monthly Routine:** Fast for 12-16 hours before working up to longer fasts. When you're ready, try a 24-hour water-only fast. Then, work your way up to 36-hour or longer fasts. It helps to have a good dinner the night before beginning a fast!

## PERSONAL STORIES AND TESTIMONIALS

Let's explore the journey of Rachel, who found balance and fulfillment through a holistic routine.

**CASE STUDY: Rachel's Balanced Life**

A busy Silicon Valley executive and single woman, Rachel often felt overwhelmed by her job and personal life demands. She struggled with stress, poor eating habits, and a sense of spiritual disconnection. Seeking a more balanced and fulfilling life, she decided to make some changes.

She started by setting aside time each morning for

prayer and meditation, using this time to set her intentions for the day. Rachel also began planning her meals more thoughtfully, focusing on whole foods that provided essential nutrients and aligned with her spiritual values. She incorporated physical activity into her routine, choosing yoga and walking as her preferred forms of exercise.

Rachel began giving thanks before meals, paying full attention to the flavors and textures of her food. She also kept a gratitude journal, reflecting on the blessings in her life and expressing gratitude for the nourishment she received.

Over time, Rachel noticed significant improvements in her physical, mental, and spiritual well-being. She felt more energized, less stressed, and more connected to her Jewish faith. Rachel's journey highlights the impact of integrating diet with spiritual practices and creating a holistic routine that supports overall health and fulfillment.

## PRACTICAL GUIDELINES FOR MAINTAINING BALANCE

Maintaining a balanced routine supporting physical and spiritual health requires consistency and mindfulness. Here are some practical guidelines to help you keep this balance:

**1. Consistency is Key:** Establish a consistent routine that includes time for diet, exercise, prayer, and meditation. Consistency helps create habits that support long-term well-being.

**2. Listen to Your Body:** Listen to your body's signals and adjust your routine as needed. Listen to your hunger cues, energy levels, and any signs of stress or fatigue.

**3. Stay Flexible:** While consistency is important, it's

also essential to remain flexible and adapt your routine to accommodate changes in your schedule or unexpected events.

**4. Seek Support:** Surround yourself with a supportive community that shares your values and goals. This could be a faith community, a fitness group, or a circle of friends who encourage and support your holistic approach to health.

**5. Reflect and Adjust:** Regularly reflect on your routine and adjust as needed. Consider how each aspect of your routine supports your well-being and make changes to enhance balance and harmony.

## SPIRITUAL INSIGHTS FROM A BALANCED LIFE

Integrating diet and exercise with spiritual practices can provide new insights and enhance well-being. Here are some spiritual insights that can be gained from a balanced life:

**1. Presence and Awareness:** A balanced routine fosters presence and awareness, helping you stay grounded in the present moment and attuned to your body's needs. This mindfulness can enhance spiritual practices and deepen your connection to the divine.

**2. Gratitude and Appreciation:** Practicing gratitude for your food and the nourishment it provides can deepen your sense of appreciation for the blessings in your life. This gratitude can enhance your overall well-being and promote a positive outlook.

**3. Harmony and Balance:** A holistic routine promotes harmony and balance in your life. This balance can enhance your overall health and spiritual well-being, creating a more conducive environment for spiritual growth.

**4. Purpose and Fulfillment:** Integrating diet, fasting,

and exercise with spiritual practices can provide a sense of purpose and fulfillment. It helps you align your daily activities with your higher purpose and focus on your spiritual goals.

May your journey be a good one!

# REFLECTIONS

As we draw to the end of *Harmony Within: Unlocking the Secrets of Holistic Wellness*, it's clear that the journey to holistic health involves much more than just eating the right foods, fasting, meditating, or engaging in physical exercise.

It is about embracing a lifestyle that honors your physical body, mind, and spiritual essence, creating a harmonious balance and supporting overall well-being. For most of us, it means devoting more time to spiritual practices such as prayer, fasting, and reading the Bible. We must program our minds and DNA to connect with the Holy Spirit.

Adopting regular focused meditation and fasting involves breaking ingrained habits for most Westerners, who are often locked into a consensus reality that does not prioritize spirituality.

In the New Testament, Jesus was not alone in performing miraculous healings; his disciples performed similar feats witnessed by hundreds of people. However, there is an instance when the disciples failed to cast a demon out of a boy who was suffering terrible seizures. After Jesus cast the demon out, Jesus and the disciples went into the boy's house with the boy's father.

> And when He had come into the house, His disciples asked Him privately, "Why could we not cast it out?"
>
> So He said to them, "This kind can come out by nothing but prayer and fasting." —**Mark 9:28-29 (NKJV)**

With discipline, miraculous healing is within our reach. Spiritual practice can improve any physical condition. We are ultimately eternal spirits in temple bodies for our time on this Earth.

In this book, we explored the interconnectedness of diet, fasting, exercise, and spirituality. Here are the key insights we discussed:

1. Unity of Body-Mind-Spirit
2. Mindful Eating and Spiritual Well-being
3. Sound Healing
4. Diet and Mental Health
5. Spiritual Practices and Cancer Treatment
6. How Diet Affects the Spiritual Life
7. Integrating Meditation with Diet and Exercise
8. Fasting for Spiritual Well-being
9. The Power of Community
10. Cultural and Traditional Influences
11. Science of Gratitude and Well-being
12. Role of Prayer and Intention
13. Integrating Diet and Exercise with Spiritual Practices

## EMBRACE THE JOURNEY

Your journey to holistic health is not a daunting task but a personal and unique experience that you have the power to shape. It's about making conscious choices that respect your body, liberate your mind, and nurture your spirit. You will create new personal values. By embracing the practices we've discussed, you're not just adopting a lifestyle but building a foundation that supports your physical, mental, and spiritual well-being.

The path to health and spirituality is not about striving for unattainable perfection but about embracing progress. It's about making small, consistent changes that align with your goals and values. Whether starting your day with a morning prayer, practicing mindful eating, or engaging in regular physical activity, each step brings you closer to a more balanced and fulfilling life.

## FINAL THOUGHTS

As you continue your unique journey, I encourage you to keep an open heart and a curious mind. Explore new practices, seek support from your community, and remain flexible in your approach. Remember, the journey to holistic health is a personal and unique experience, and it's crucial to find what works best for you. Your journey is unique, but you are not alone in it.

Thank you for accompanying me on this journey. May your path be filled with health, peace, and spiritual fulfillment. Embrace the interconnectedness of your body, mind, and spirit, and discover its tremendous impact on your life.

# SHARING THE SPIRIT

THANK YOU

Now that you are on the path to inner peace and harmony, it's time to share your newfound knowledge. By leaving your honest opinion of this book on Amazon, you'll guide other seekers to the help they need and inspire their journey toward inner peace.

Your contribution is of immense value. By sharing our knowledge, we collectively advance consciousness, and your review is a significant part of this process.

Please take a moment to leave a review on Amazon. Your words can make a difference in someone's journey toward body-mind-spirit integration and inner peace.

Click here to leave a review. Or point your phone at the QR code.

Thank you!

# BIBLIOGRAPHY

**Books and Articles:**

Algoe, S. B., Haidt, J., & Gable, S. L. (2008). Beyond reciprocity: Gratitude and relationships in everyday life. *Emotion*, 8(3), 425-429.

Cedars-Sinai. (2024). Researchers look to fasting as a next step in cancer treatment. Cedars-Sinai. Retrieved June 6, 2024, from https://www. cedars-sinai.org/newsroom/researchers-look-to-fasting-as-a-next-step-in-cancer-treatment/ (accessed June 14, 2024)

Collins, N., Phillips, N.L.H., Reich, L. *et al.* Epigenetic Consequences of Adversity and Intervention Throughout the Lifespan: Implications for Public Policy and Healthcare. *ADV RES SCI* **1**, 205–216 (2020). https://doi.org/10.1007/s42844-020-00015-5

Emmons, R. A., & McCullough, M. E. (2003). Counting blessings versus burdens: An experimental investigation of gratitude and subjective well-being in daily life. *Journal of Personality and Social Psychology*, 84(2), 377-389.

Freeman, M. P., Hibbeln, J. R., Wisner, K. L., et al. (2011). Omega-3 fatty acids: evidence basis for treatment and future research in psychiatry. *Journal of Clinical Psychiatry*, 72(8), 1054-1062.

Garyaev, P. P. (2013). *Wave genetics: Theory and practice.* Moscow: Research Institute of Wave Genetics.

Gilbody, S., Lightfoot, T., & Sheldon, T. (2007). Is low folate a risk factor for depression? A meta-analysis and exploration of heterogeneity. *Journal of Epidemiology & Community Health*, 61(7), 631-637. https://doi.org/10.1136/jech.2006.050385

Ginde, A. A., Mansbach, J. M., & Camargo, C. A. (2009). Association between serum 25-hydroxyvitamin D level and upper respiratory tract infection in the Third National Health and Nutrition Examination Survey. *Archives of Internal Medicine, 169*(4), 384-390. https://doi.org/10.1001/archinternmed.2008.560

Goyal, M., Singh, S., Sibinga, E. M. S., et al. (2014). Meditation programs for psychological stress and well-being: a systematic review and meta-analysis. *JAMA Internal Medicine*, 174(3), 357-368.

Hagelin, J. S., Rainforth, M. V., Orme-Johnson, D. W., Cavanaugh, K. L., Alexander, C. N., Shatkin, S. F., Davies, J. L., Hughes, A. O., & Ross, E. (1999). Reduced violent crime in Washington, DC: Effects of group practice of the Transcendental Meditation program on preventing violent crime in Washington, DC: Results of the National Demonstration Project, June–July 1993. Maharishi International University. Retrieved from https://research.miu.edu/maharishi-effect/reduced-violent-crime-in-washington-dc (accessed June 8, 2024)

Harvard Health. (n.d.). Walking just 4,000 steps a day can help you live longer. Retrieved from https://www.health.harvard.edu (accessed June 8, 2024).

Harvard Medical School. (2015). Music as medicine: The impact of healing harmonies. Retrieved June 14, 2024, from https://hms.harvard.edu/sites/default/files/assets/Sites/Longwood_Seminars/Longwood%20Seminar%20Music%20Reading%20Pack.pdf (accessed June 14, 2024)

Jaušovec, N., & Habe, K. (2003). The "Mozart Effect": An electroencephalographic analysis employing the methods of induced event-related desynchronization/synchronization and event-related partial coherence. *Brain Topography*, **16**(2), 73-84.Lad, V. (1984). Ayurveda: The Science of Self-Healing. The Ayurvedic Press.

Johns Hopkins Medicine. (2024). Intermittent fasting: What is it, and how does it work? *Johns Hopkins Medicine*. Retrieved June 6, 2024, from https://www.hopkinsmedicine.org/health/wellness-and-prevention/intermittent-fasting (accessed June 14, 2024)

Kanduri, C., Raijas, P., Ahvenainen, M., Philips, A. K., Ukkola-Vuoti, L., Lähdesmäki, H., & Järvelä, I. (2015). The effect of listening to music on human transcriptome. *PeerJ, 3*, e830. https://doi.org/10.7717/peerj.830 (accessed June 14, 2024)

Leonard Davis School of Gerontology. (2018, November 21). *Fasting for 72 hours can reset your entire immune system.* The Source. https://thesource.com/2018/11/21/fasting-for-72-hours-can-reset-your-entire-immune-system/ (accessed Jun 8, 2024).

Levin, J. (2011). Religion and mental health: Theory and research. *International Journal of Applied Psychoanalytic Studies*, 8(3), 244-251.

Mayo Clinic. (n.d.). Walking: Trim your waistline, improve your health. Retrieved from https://www.mayoclinic.org (accessed June 8, 2024).

McTaggart, L. (2007). The Intention Experiment: Using Your Thoughts to Change Your Life and the World. Free Press.

Peiying, Y., Richard, W. W., & Lorenzo, C. (2022). Understanding the link between sugar and cancer: An examination of the preclinical and clinical evidence. *Cancers*, 14(24), 6042. https://doi.org/10.3390/cancers14246042

Radin, D. (1997). *The Conscious Universe: The scientific truth of psychic phenomena.* HarperEdge.

Rea, C., Lonati, V., Luciani, A., & Ghidini, A. (2023). Vitamin D3 and COVID-19 outcomes: An umbrella review of systematic reviews and meta-analyses. *Antioxidants, 12*(2), 247. https://doi.org/10.3390/antiox12020247

Reynolds, E. H. (2002). Folic acid, ageing, depression, and dementia. *BMJ*, 324(7352), 1512-1515. https://doi.org/10.1136/bmj.324.7352.1512 (accessed June 14, 2024)

Sansone, R. A., & Sansone, L. A. (2010). Gratitude and well-being: The benefits of appreciation. *Psychiatry* (Edgmont), 7(11), 18-22.

Sarkar, A., Lehto, S. M., Harty, S., & Dinan, T. G. (2016). Psychobiotics and the manipulation of bacteria–gut-brain signals. *Trends in Neurosciences*, 39(11), 763-781.

Southwick, S. M., & Charney, D. S. (2012). Resilience: The Science of Mastering Life's Greatest Challenges. Cambridge University Press.

Targ, R. (2014, January 14). Changing our DNA through mind control? *Scientific American.* Retrieved from https://www.scientificamerican.com/article/changing-our-dna-through-mind-control/

Tessier A, Cortese M, Yuan C, et al. Consumption of Olive Oil and Diet Quality and Risk of Dementia-Related Death. *JAMA Netw Open.* 2024;7(5):e2410021. doi:10.1001/jamanetworkopen.2024.10021

Tiller, W. A. (2007). Psychoenergetic Science: A Second Copernican-Scale Revolution. Pavior Publishing.

Trichopoulou, A., Bamia, C., & Trichopoulos, D. (2014). Mediterranean diet and survival among patients with coronary heart disease in Greece. *Archives of Internal Medicine*, 165(8), 929-935.

Willcox, D. C., Willcox, B. J., & Suzuki, M. (2009). The Okinawa diet: Healthy aging and longevity. *Asian Pacific Journal of Clinical Nutrition*, 18(3), 481-484.

Wood, A. M., Froh, J. J., & Geraghty, A. W. (2010). Gratitude and well-being: A review and theoretical integration. *Clinical Psychology Review*, 30(7), 890-905.

Wood, A. M., Joseph, S., Lloyd, J., & Atkins, S. (2009). Gratitude influences sleep through the mechanism of pre-sleep cognitions. *Journal of Psychosomatic Research*, 66(1), 43-48.

**Scriptural References (NIV):**

**Philippians 4:6-7:** *"Do not be anxious about anything, but in every situation, by prayer and petition, with thanksgiving, present your requests to God. And the peace of God, which transcends all understanding, will guard your hearts and your minds in Christ Jesus."*

**James 5:16:** *"Therefore confess your sins to each other and pray for each other so that you may be healed. The prayer of a righteous person is powerful and effective."*

**Matthew 4:2:** *"After fasting forty days and forty nights, he was hungry."*

**Deuteronomy 14:3-21:** This passage details the dietary laws given to the Israelites, outlining clean and unclean foods.

**Quran 5:3:** *"Prohibited to you are dead animals, blood, the flesh of swine, and that which has been dedicated to other than Allah, and those animals killed by strangling or by a violent blow or by a headlong fall or by the goring of horns, and those from which a wild animal has eaten, except what you [are able to] slaughter [before its death], and those which are sacrificed on stone altars, and [prohibited is] that you seek decision through divining arrows. That is grave disobedience. This day those who disbelieve have despaired of [defeating] your religion; so fear them not, but fear Me. This day I have perfected for you your religion and completed My favor upon you and have approved for you Islam as religion. But whoever is forced by severe hunger with no inclination to sin then indeed, Allah is Forgiving and Merciful."*

**Matthew 6:16-18:** *"When you fast, do not look somber as the hypocrites do, for they disfigure their faces to show others they are fasting. Truly I tell you, they have received their reward in full. But when you fast, put oil on your head and wash your face, so that it will not be obvious to others that you are fasting, but only to your Father, who is unseen; and your Father, who sees what is done in secret, will reward you."*

**Acts 2:42:** *"They devoted themselves to the apostles' teaching and to fellowship, to the breaking of bread and to prayer."*

**Galatians 6:2:** *"Carry each other's burdens, and in this way, you will fulfill the law of Christ."*

**Hebrews 10:24-25:** *"And let us consider how we may spur one another on toward love and good deeds, not giving up meeting together, as some are in the habit of doing, but encouraging one another—and all the more as you see the Day approaching."*

**Genesis 1:29:** *"Then God said, 'I give you every seed-bearing plant on the face of the whole earth and every tree that has fruit with seed in it. They will be yours for food.'"*

**Proverbs 25:27:** *"It is not good to eat too much honey, nor is it honorable to search out matters that are too deep."*

# BIBLIOGRAPHY

**1 Corinthians 10:31:** *"So whether you eat or drink or whatever you do, do it all for the glory of God."*

**Matthew 6:11:** *"Give us today our daily bread."*

# APPENDIX: DAILY MEDITATIONS

DAILY MEDITATIONS

**1. Jeremiah 29:11 (NIV): "For I know the plans I have for you," declares the Lord, "plans to prosper you and not to harm you, plans to give you hope and a future."**

God's plans for us are always for our good. Even when we face challenges, we can trust that His intentions are to prosper us and give us hope. Today, take comfort in knowing that God has a purpose and plan for your life, one filled with hope and promise.

**2. Psalm 23:1 (NIV): "The Lord is my shepherd, I lack nothing."**

The Lord, as our shepherd, provides for all our needs. In Him, we find everything we need for a fulfilling life. Today, rest assured that you will lack nothing with God as your shepherd.

**3. Philippians 4:13 (NIV): "I can do all this through him who gives me strength."**

Christ is the source of our strength, enabling us to overcome any challenge. Today, draw on His strength to face your difficulties with confidence and courage.

**4. Matthew 6:34 (NIV): "Therefore do not worry about tomorrow, for tomorrow will worry about itself. Each day has enough trouble of its own."**

Worrying about the future only adds to today's burdens. Trust in God's provision for each day and focus on the present. Today, practice living in the moment, trusting God to care for your tomorrows.

**5. Romans 8:28 (NIV): "And we know that in all things God works for the good of those who love him, who have been called according to his purpose."**

God orchestrates everything for the good of His people. We can trust that He works for our benefit, even in difficult times. Today, take comfort in knowing God uses every circumstance for your good.

**6. Isaiah 40:31 (NIV): "But those who hope in the Lord will renew their strength. They will soar on wings like eagles; they will run and not grow weary, they will walk and not be faint."**

Hoping in the Lord brings renewed strength and vitality. Trusting in Him lifts us above our challenges. Today, place your hope in God and experience the renewal of your strength.

**7. Psalm 46:10 (NIV): "He says, 'Be still, and know that I am God; I will be exalted among the nations, I will be exalted in the earth.'"**

Being still before God allows us to recognize His sovereignty and power. Today, take a moment to be still and acknowledge God's greatness, knowing He is exalted above all.

**8. John 14:27 (NIV): "Peace I leave with you; my peace I give you. I do not give to you as the world gives.**

Do not let your hearts be troubled and do not be afraid."

Jesus offers us His peace, unlike anything the world can offer. Today, accept His peace and let it calm your heart and mind.

**9. Philippians 4:6-7 (NIV): "Do not be anxious about anything, but in every situation, by prayer and petition, with thanksgiving, present your requests to God. And the peace of God, which transcends all understanding, will guard your hearts and your minds in Christ Jesus."**

Prayer and thanksgiving are antidotes to anxiety. Presenting our concerns to God brings His peace into our hearts. Today, practice giving your anxieties to God through prayer, and let His peace guard your heart and mind.

**10. Matthew 11:28 (NIV): "Come to me, all you who are weary and burdened, and I will give you rest."**

Jesus invites us to come to Him with our burdens, promising rest. Today, bring your worries and burdens to Jesus and rest in His presence.

**11. Proverbs 3:5-6 (NIV): "Trust in the Lord with all your heart and lean not on your own understanding; in all your ways submit to him, and he will make your paths straight."**

Trusting in the Lord involves submitting our ways to Him and relying on His understanding. Today, trust God with all your heart, acknowledging Him in every area of your life.

**12. Romans 12:2 (NIV): "Do not conform to the pattern of this world, but be transformed by the renewing of your mind. Then you will be able to test and approve what God's will is—his good, pleasing and perfect will."**

Transformation begins with renewing our minds. By

focusing on God's truth, we align ourselves with His will. Today, seek to renew your mind through God's Word and be transformed to understand His will.

**13. Psalm 37:4 (NIV): "Take delight in the Lord, and he will give you the desires of your heart."**

Delighting in the Lord aligns our desires with His. Today, find joy in God's presence and trust that He will fulfill the desires of your heart.

**14. Isaiah 41:10 (NIV): "So do not fear, for I am with you; do not be dismayed, for I am your God. I will strengthen you and help you; I will uphold you with my righteous right hand."**

God's presence dispels fear and brings strength. Today, rely on His promise to be with you, strengthen and uphold you.

**15. 1 Peter 5:7 (NIV): "Cast all your anxiety on him because he cares for you."**

God cares deeply for us and invites us to cast our anxieties on Him. Today, release your worries to God, trusting His care and provision.

**16. Psalm 23:4 (NIV): "Even though I walk through the darkest valley, I will fear no evil, for you are with me; your rod and your staff, they comfort me."**

God's presence in our darkest moments brings comfort and dispels fear. Today, find solace in knowing God walks with you through every valley, offering His comfort and support.

**17. Philippians 4:19 (NIV): "And my God will meet all your needs according to the riches of his glory in Christ Jesus."**

God promises to supply all our needs from His abundant riches in Christ. Today, trust in God's provision, knowing He is faithful to meet every need you have, according to His glorious riches.

**18. John 16:33 (NIV): "I have told you these things, so that in me you may have peace. In this world you will have trouble. But take heart! I have overcome the world."**

Jesus assures us of peace in Him despite the troubles of the world. His victory over the world gives us hope and courage. Today, take heart in Jesus' triumph, finding peace in His words and strength in His victory.

**19. Romans 8:38-39 (NIV): "For I am convinced that neither death nor life, neither angels nor demons, neither the present nor the future, nor any powers, neither height nor depth, nor anything else in all creation, will be able to separate us from the love of God that is in Christ Jesus our Lord."**

God's love for us is unwavering and unbreakable. Nothing in all creation can separate us from His love. Today, rest assured of God's steadfast love and let it be your source of comfort and strength in all circumstances.

**20. James 4:8 (NIV): "Come near to God and he will come near to you. Wash your hands, you sinners, and purify your hearts, you double-minded."**

Drawing near to God involves repentance and seeking purity. As we approach Him with sincerity, He draws closer to us. Today, take steps to cleanse your heart and mind, seeking a deeper and more intimate relationship with God.

**21. 1 Corinthians 16:13-14 (NIV): "Be on your guard; stand firm in the faith; be courageous; be strong. Do everything in love."**

Standing firm in faith requires vigilance, courage, and strength, but it must all be rooted in love. Today, resolve to be steadfast in your faith, courageous in your actions, and loving in all you do, reflecting God's character in every aspect of your life.

**22. Psalm 46:1 (NIV): "God is our refuge and strength, an ever-present help in trouble."**

In times of trouble, God is our refuge and strength. His presence is a constant source of help and comfort. Today, turn to God with your worries and fears, knowing He is always ready to support and protect you.

**23. Philippians 2:3-4 (NIV): "Do nothing out of selfish ambition or vain conceit. Rather, in humility value others above yourselves, not looking to your own interests but each of you to the interests of the others."**

Humility and selflessness are vital to living in harmony with others. By valuing others and considering their needs, we reflect Christ's love. Today, practice putting others first, seeking to serve and uplift those around you.

**24. Psalm 91:1-2 (NIV): "Whoever dwells in the shelter of the Most High will rest in the shadow of the Almighty. I will say of the Lord, 'He is my refuge and my fortress, my God, in whom I trust.'"**

Dwelling in God's presence brings security and peace. As we rest in His shadow, we find refuge and strength. Today, make God's presence your dwelling place, trusting Him as your fortress and protector.

**25. Romans 12:12 (NIV): "Be joyful in hope, patient in affliction, faithful in prayer."**

Joy, patience, and faithfulness are essential for enduring life's challenges. By maintaining hope, patience, and a strong prayer life, we remain connected to God. Today, embody these qualities, trusting in God's faithfulness and timing.

**26. Isaiah 40:29 (NIV): "He gives strength to the weary and increases the power of the weak."**

God's strength is available to us when we feel weary and weak. He empowers us to keep going. Today, rely on God's strength to carry you through difficult times, knowing that His power is made perfect in your weakness.

**27. John 14:1 (NIV): "Do not let your hearts be troubled. You believe in God; believe also in me."**

Jesus encourages us to trust in Him and not let our hearts be troubled. Belief in God and Jesus brings peace and assurance. Today, trust Jesus, allowing Him to calm your troubled heart and fill you with peace.

**28. 2 Corinthians 12:9 (NIV): "But he said to me, 'My grace is sufficient for you, for my power is made perfect in weakness.' Therefore I will boast all the more gladly about my weaknesses, so that Christ's power may rest on me."**

God's grace is sufficient for all our needs. His power is displayed in our weakness. Today, embrace your weaknesses, knowing they are opportunities for Christ's power to be revealed.

**29. Psalm 37:5 (NIV): "Commit your way to the Lord; trust in him and he will do this."**

Committing our way to the Lord involves trusting Him with our plans and desires. When we do, He acts on our behalf. Today, commit your path to God, trusting Him to lead and guide you according to His will.

**30. Hebrews 10:24-25 (NIV): "And let us consider how we may spur one another on toward love and good deeds, not giving up meeting together, as some are in the habit of doing, but encouraging one another—and all the more as you see the Day approaching."**

Community and encouragement are vital for spiritual growth. By gathering together and spurring one another on, we strengthen our faith. Today, seek opportunities to connect with and encourage your faith community.

**31. Isaiah 55:8-9 (NIV): "For my thoughts are not your thoughts, neither are your ways my ways," declares the Lord. "As the heavens are higher than the earth, so are my ways higher than your ways and my thoughts than your thoughts."**

God's thoughts and ways are far beyond our understanding, and His perspective is infinitely higher. Today, trust in God's wisdom and plan, knowing His ways are always best, even when you don't understand.

**32. Proverbs 4:23 (NIV): "Above all else, guard your heart, for everything you do flows from it."**

Guarding our hearts is crucial because it influences all aspects of our lives. Protecting our hearts from negative influences allows God's love to flow through us. Remember what you allow into your heart today, keeping it pure and focused on God.

**33. 1 Peter 4:8 (NIV): "Above all, love each other deeply, because love covers over a multitude of sins."**

Deep, sincere love has the power to cover and heal many wrongs. By loving others deeply, we reflect God's grace and forgiveness. Today, love others deeply and unconditionally, extending grace and forgiveness in all your relationships.

**34. Matthew 28:20 (NIV): "And surely I am with you always, to the very end of the age."**

Jesus' promise to be with us always provides comfort and assurance. Today, remember that you are never alone; Jesus is with you, guiding and supporting you through every moment of your life.

**35. Proverbs 17:17 (NIV): "A friend loves at all times, and a brother is born for a time of adversity."**

True friendship and brotherhood are steadfast, especially in adversity. Today, be a faithful friend and support to others, loving them through all circumstances and challenges.

**36. John 15:12 (NIV): "My command is this: Love each other as I have loved you."**

Jesus commands us to love others as He has loved us. Today, reflect on Jesus's sacrificial love and strive to love others with the same selflessness and compassion.

**37. Psalm 119:105 (NIV): "Your word is a lamp for my feet, a light on my path."**

God's Word provides guidance and direction for our lives. Today, turn to the Bible for wisdom and guidance, allowing it to light your way.

**38. Hebrews 12:1 (NIV): "Therefore, since we are surrounded by such a great cloud of witnesses, let us throw off everything that hinders and the sin that so easily entangles. And let us run with perseverance the race marked out for us."**

The encouragement of those who have gone before us inspires perseverance. Today, shed any hindrances and sin and run your race with determination, encouraged by the faithful examples of others.

**39. 2 Corinthians 4:16 (NIV): "Therefore we do not lose heart. Though outwardly we are wasting away, yet inwardly we are being renewed day by day."**

Despite physical decay, God's Spirit renews our inner self daily. Today, focus on the inward renewal God provides and do not lose heart in the face of outward challenges.

**40. Psalm 34:18 (NIV): "The Lord is close to the brokenhearted and saves those who are crushed in spirit."**

God's nearness comforts the brokenhearted and the

crushed in spirit. Today, seek His presence and healing, knowing He is incredibly close to you in times of sorrow and distress.

**41. Romans 5:8 (NIV): "But God demonstrates his own love for us in this: While we were still sinners, Christ died for us."**

God's love is demonstrated through Christ's sacrifice for us, even while we were sinners. Today, reflect on the depth of God's love and let it inspire gratitude and a desire to live for Him.

**42. Psalm 91:4 (NIV): "He will cover you with his feathers, and under his wings you will find refuge; his faithfulness will be your shield and rampart."**

God's protection and faithfulness are like a sheltering wing. Rest under God's protective care today, finding refuge and safety in His faithfulness.

**43. Isaiah 43:2 (NIV): "When you pass through the waters, I will be with you; and when you pass through the rivers, they will not sweep over you. When you walk through the fire, you will not be burned; the flames will not set you ablaze."**

God promises to be with us in the midst of trials. Today, remember that no matter your challenges, God is with you, protecting and guiding you.

**44. Matthew 5:14 (NIV): "You are the light of the world. A town built on a hill cannot be hidden."**

Jesus calls us to be the light of the world. Today, let your actions reflect the light of Christ, shining brightly in a world that needs His love and truth.

**45. Psalm 121:1-2 (NIV): "I lift up my eyes to the mountains—where does my help come from? My help comes from the Lord, the Maker of heaven and earth."**

Recognizing that our help comes from God brings peace

and confidence. Today, lift your eyes to God, the Maker of heaven and earth, and trust in His unfailing help and support.

**46. John 3:16 (NIV): "For God so loved the world that he gave his one and only Son, that whoever believes in him shall not perish but have eternal life."**

God's love for the world is demonstrated through the gift of His Son. Today, reflect on the magnitude of God's love and the promise of eternal life for those who believe in Jesus.

**47. Ephesians 6:11 (NIV): "Put on the full armor of God, so that you can take your stand against the devil's schemes."**

Putting on the whole armor of God equips us to stand against spiritual attacks. Today, prepare yourself with truth, righteousness, faith, and the Word of God, ready to face any challenge.

**48. 1 Corinthians 10:13 (NIV): "No temptation has overtaken you except what is common to mankind. And God is faithful; he will not let you be tempted beyond what you can bear. But when you are tempted, he will also provide a way out so that you can endure it."**

God's faithfulness ensures that we will not face temptations beyond our ability to withstand. Today, trust in God's provision for strength and a way out of temptation.

**49. Psalm 18:2 (NIV): "The Lord is my rock, my fortress and my deliverer; my God is my rock, in whom I take refuge, my shield and the horn of my salvation, my stronghold."**

God is our unshakeable rock and fortress. Today, take refuge in Him, trusting His strength and deliverance in times of trouble.

**50. 2 Timothy 1:7 (NIV): "For the Spirit God gave us**

does not make us timid, but gives us power, love and self-discipline."

The Holy Spirit empowers us with courage, love, and self-discipline. Today, rely on the Spirit's power to overcome fear and live boldly in faith.

**51. Psalm 55:22 (NIV): "Cast your cares on the Lord and he will sustain you; he will never let the righteous be shaken."**

God sustains those who cast their cares on Him. Today, give your burdens to the Lord and trust His unwavering support and sustenance.

**52. James 1:2-3 (NIV): "Consider it pure joy, my brothers and sisters, whenever you face trials of many kinds, because you know that the testing of your faith produces perseverance."**

Trials and challenges strengthen our faith and perseverance. Today, view your trials as opportunities for growth and joy, knowing God is refining your faith.

**53. Psalm 121:7-8 (NIV): "The Lord will keep you from all harm—he will watch over your life; the Lord will watch over your coming and going both now and forevermore."**

God's watchful care protects us from harm. Today, take comfort in God's constant presence and protection over your life.

**54. Matthew 6:33 (NIV): "But seek first his kingdom and his righteousness, and all these things will be given to you as well."**

Prioritizing God's kingdom and righteousness brings provision for all our needs. Today, seek God's kingdom, trusting Him to provide for everything else.

**55. Psalm 34:4 (NIV): "I sought the Lord, and he answered me; he delivered me from all my fears."**

Seeking the Lord leads to deliverance from fear. Today, turn to God with your fears, trusting Him to bring you peace and freedom.

**56. 1 John 4:18 (NIV): "There is no fear in love. But perfect love drives out fear, because fear has to do with punishment. The one who fears is not made perfect in love."**

God's perfect love eliminates fear, replacing it with security and peace. Today, embrace His ideal love, allowing it to cast out all fear from your heart and mind, and will enable you to live confidently in His love.

**57. Psalm 37:7 (NIV): "Be still before the Lord and wait patiently for him; do not fret when people succeed in their ways, when they carry out their wicked schemes."**

Waiting patiently for the Lord involves trusting His timing and justice. Today, practice stillness and patience, trusting God to handle situations and people around you without fretting over the apparent successes of the wicked.

**58. John 10:10 (NIV): "The thief comes only to steal and kill and destroy; I have come that they may have life, and have it to the full."**

Jesus came to give us abundant life, in contrast to the destruction brought by the thief. Today, embrace the fullness of life that Jesus offers, seeking to live abundantly in His grace and love.

**59. Proverbs 18:10 (NIV): "The name of the Lord is a fortified tower; the righteous run to it and are safe."**

The Lord's name is a place of safety and protection for the righteous. Today, run to God in times of trouble, finding safety and refuge in His mighty name.

**60. Romans 8:1 (NIV): "Therefore, there is now no condemnation for those who are in Christ Jesus."**

In Christ, we are free from condemnation. His grace covers our sins and makes us righteous. Today, live in the freedom and confidence that comes from knowing you are no longer condemned but forgiven and loved by God.

**61. Psalm 100:4 (NIV): "Enter his gates with thanksgiving and his courts with praise; give thanks to him and praise his name."**

Approaching God with thanksgiving and praise opens our hearts to His presence. Today, enter God's presence with a grateful heart, lifting praise and thanks for His goodness and love.

**62. Matthew 7:7 (NIV): "Ask and it will be given to you; seek and you will find; knock and the door will be opened to you."**

Jesus encourages us to pray, promising our efforts will be rewarded. Today, approach God confidently, asking, seeking, and knocking, knowing He hears and responds to your prayers.

**63. Isaiah 54:17 (NIV): "No weapon forged against you will prevail, and you will refute every tongue that accuses you. This is the heritage of the servants of the Lord, and this is their vindication from me," declares the Lord.**

God's protection ensures that no weapon or accusation against us will succeed. Stand firm in your faith today, confident in God's promise to protect and vindicate you against all adversities.

**64. Psalm 118:24 (NIV): "The Lord has done it this very day; let us rejoice today and be glad."**

Rejoicing the day the Lord has made brings a positive and grateful attitude to our daily life. Today, choose to rejoice and be glad, recognizing God's handiwork in your life and embracing His blessings with joy.

**65. Hebrews 4:16 (NIV): "Let us then approach God's throne of grace with confidence, so that we may receive mercy and find grace to help us in our time of need."**

Approaching God's throne confidently allows us to receive His mercy and grace. Today, boldly come before God with your needs and trust that He will provide the help and grace you seek.

**66. Proverbs 3:6 (NIV): "In all your ways submit to him, and he will make your paths straight."**

Submitting our ways to God ensures that He will direct our paths. Today, align your plans and actions with God's will, trusting He will guide you on the right path and make your way straight.

**67. Romans 12:1 (NIV): "Therefore, I urge you, brothers and sisters, in view of God's mercy, to offer your bodies as a living sacrifice, holy and pleasing to God—this is your true and proper worship."**

Offering ourselves as living sacrifices is our actual act of worship. Today, dedicate your body, mind, and spirit to God, living in a holy and pleasing way to Him as an expression of your worship.

**68. John 15:5 (NIV): "I am the vine; you are the branches. If you remain in me and I in you, you will bear much fruit; apart from me you can do nothing."**

Remaining in Jesus ensures our fruitfulness. Today, focus on strengthening your relationship with Him, knowing that apart from Him, we can do nothing, but with Him, we can bear much fruit.

**69. 2 Corinthians 5:7 (NIV): "For we live by faith, not by sight."**

Living by faith means trusting God even when we cannot see the outcome. Today, walk by faith, trusting in

God's promises and plan for your life, even when the path is unclear.

**70. Psalm 23:6 (NIV): "Surely your goodness and love will follow me all the days of my life, and I will dwell in the house of the Lord forever."**

God's goodness and love follow us throughout our lives. Today, take comfort in His promise of everlasting love and the assurance that you will dwell in His house forever.

**71. Matthew 5:16 (NIV): "In the same way, let your light shine before others, that they may see your good deeds and glorify your Father in heaven."**

Letting our light shine brings glory to God. Today, strive to do good deeds and live in a way that reflects God's love so that others may see and glorify Him.

**72. Psalm 19:14 (NIV): "May these words of my mouth and this meditation of my heart be pleasing in your sight, Lord, my Rock and my Redeemer."**

Seeking to please God with our words and thoughts aligns our hearts with His will. Today, focus on speaking and thinking in ways pleasing God, our Rock and Redeemer.

**73. Ephesians 3:20 (NIV): "Now to him who is able to do immeasurably more than all we ask or imagine, according to his power that is at work within us."**

God's power working within us can accomplish more than we can imagine. Today, trust in His limitless power to do great things in and through your life beyond your wildest dreams.

**74. Psalm 37:23-24 (NIV): "The Lord makes firm the steps of the one who delights in him; though he may stumble, he will not fall, for the Lord upholds him with his hand."**

God upholds and guides those who delight in Him. Today, rejoice in the Lord and trust He will firm your steps and uphold you even when you stumble.

**75. 1 Thessalonians 5:16-18 (NIV): "Rejoice always, pray continually, give thanks in all circumstances; for this is God's will for you in Christ Jesus."**

Rejoicing, praying, and giving thanks in all circumstances reflect God's will for us. Today, practice these three attitudes, finding joy, prayerfulness, and gratitude in every situation, knowing that it aligns you with God's will.

**76. Psalm 28:7 (NIV): "The Lord is my strength and my shield; my heart trusts in him, and he helps me. My heart leaps for joy, and with my song I praise him."**

God is our strength and shield, bringing joy and help to those who trust Him. Today, trust in the Lord with all your heart, find joy in His help and strength, and lift songs of praise to Him.

**77. John 8:12 (NIV): "When Jesus spoke again to the people, he said, 'I am the light of the world. Whoever follows me will never walk in darkness, but will have the light of life.'"**

Following Jesus brings light into our lives, dispelling darkness. Today, follow Him closely, embracing His light and allowing it to guide you, keeping you from the darkness of sin and confusion.

**78. Psalm 56:3 (NIV): "When I am afraid, I put my trust in you."**

Trusting God removes fear and brings peace. Whenever fear arises, trust God, knowing He is your protector and source of peace.

**79. 1 Corinthians 13:4-7 (NIV): "Love is patient, love is kind. It does not envy, it does not boast, it is not**

**proud. It does not dishonor others, it is not self-seeking, it is not easily angered, it keeps no record of wrongs. Love does not delight in evil but rejoices with the truth. It always protects, always trusts, always hopes, always perseveres."**

True love is patient, kind, and enduring. Today, practice this kind of love in your relationships, embodying the attributes of godly love in every interaction.

**80. Psalm 16:8 (NIV): "I keep my eyes always on the Lord. With him at my right hand, I will not be shaken."**

Keeping our eyes on the Lord brings stability and confidence. Today, focus on the Lord, knowing that His presence at your right hand will ensure that you will not be shaken by life's challenges.

**81. Colossians 3:23-24 (NIV): "Whatever you do, work at it with all your heart, as working for the Lord, not for human masters, since you know that you will receive an inheritance from the Lord as a reward. It is the Lord Christ you are serving."**

Working wholeheartedly for the Lord brings eternal rewards. Today, approach your tasks with dedication and excellence, knowing that you are serving Christ and will receive His reward.

**82. Psalm 34:8 (NIV): "Taste and see that the Lord is good; blessed is the one who takes refuge in him."**

Experiencing God's goodness brings blessing and refuge. Today, reflect on God's goodness and find shelter and blessing in His loving care.

**83. Romans 15:13 (NIV): "May the God of hope fill you with all joy and peace as you trust in him, so that you may overflow with hope by the power of the Holy Spirit."**

Trusting in God fills us with joy, peace, and hope through the Holy Spirit. Today, place your trust in God, allowing His Spirit to fill you with joy and peace, overflowing with hope in every situation.

**84. Psalm 121:3 (NIV): "He will not let your foot slip —he who watches over you will not slumber."**

God's constant vigilance ensures our safety and security. Today, trust in God's watchful care, knowing He never slumbers and protects you from slipping.

**85. James 1:22 (NIV): "Do not merely listen to the word, and so deceive yourselves. Do what it says."**

Acting on God's Word brings true transformation. Today, commit to hearing God's Word and putting it into practice, allowing it to shape your actions and character.

**86. Psalm 27:4 (NIV): "One thing I ask from the Lord, this only do I seek: that I may dwell in the house of the Lord all the days of my life, to gaze on the beauty of the Lord and to seek him in his temple."**

Desiring to dwell in God's presence brings fulfillment and joy. Today, seek to spend time in God's presence, gazing at His beauty and finding delight in communion with Him.

**87. 1 John 1:9 (NIV): "If we confess our sins, he is faithful and just and will forgive us our sins and purify us from all unrighteousness."**

Confessing our sins brings forgiveness and purification from God. Today, approach God with a repentant heart, confessing your sins and experiencing His faithful and just forgiveness.

**88. Psalm 139:23-24 (NIV): "Search me, God, and know my heart; test me and know my anxious thoughts. See if there is any offensive way in me, and lead me in the way everlasting."**

Inviting God to search our hearts leads to purification and guidance. Today, ask God to examine your heart, reveal any offensive ways, and guide you to everlasting life.

**89. 2 Corinthians 9:8 (NIV): "And God is able to bless you abundantly, so that in all things at all times, having all that you need, you will abound in every good work."**

God's abundant blessings equip us for every good work. Today, trust in God's ability to provide all you need, allowing you to abound in every good work He calls you to.

**90. Psalm 91:11 (NIV): "For he will command his angels concerning you to guard you in all your ways."**

God commands His angels to guard and protect us. Today, take comfort in the divine protection and guidance that God provides through His angels, watching over you in all your ways.

**91. Galatians 5:22-23 (NIV): "But the fruit of the Spirit is love, joy, peace, forbearance, kindness, goodness, faithfulness, gentleness and self-control. Against such things there is no law."**

The fruit of the Spirit reflects God's character in our lives. Today, seek to cultivate these attributes in your life, allowing the Holy Spirit to produce His fruit in you.

**92. Psalm 37:25 (NIV): "I was young and now I am old, yet I have never seen the righteous forsaken or their children begging bread."**

God's faithfulness ensures that the righteous are never forsaken. Today, reflect on God's consistent provision and faithfulness throughout your life, trusting Him to continue to meet your needs.

**93. 1 Peter 2:9 (NIV): "But you are a chosen people, a royal priesthood, a holy nation, God's special posses-**

sion, that you may declare the praises of him who called you out of darkness into his wonderful light."

Being chosen by God calls us to declare His praises. Today, embrace your identity as God's special possession, declaring His praises and sharing the light of His love with others.

**94. Psalm 84:10 (NIV): "Better is one day in your courts than a thousand elsewhere; I would rather be a doorkeeper in the house of my God than dwell in the tents of the wicked."**

Valuing time in God's presence over worldly pleasures brings true fulfillment. Today, prioritize spending time in God's presence, finding joy and satisfaction in Him above all else.

**95. Romans 8:18 (NIV): "I consider that our present sufferings are not worth comparing with the glory that will be revealed in us."**

The glory to be revealed far outweighs our present sufferings. Today, find hope and encouragement in the promise of future glory, knowing that God's plans for you are beyond what you can imagine.

**96. Psalm 34:7 (NIV): "The angel of the Lord encamps around those who fear him, and he delivers them."**

God's angels protect and deliver those who fear Him. Today, take comfort in knowing God's angelic protection surrounds you, keeping you safe from harm.

**97. Philippians 1:6 (NIV): "Being confident of this, that he who began a good work in you will carry it on to completion until the day of Christ Jesus."**

God's work in us will be brought to completion. Today, trust in God's ongoing work in your life, knowing He is faithful to get it to fruition in His perfect timing.

**98. Psalm 30:5 (NIV): "For his anger lasts only a moment, but his favor lasts a lifetime; weeping may stay for the night, but rejoicing comes in the morning."**

God's favor brings lifelong joy, even after times of weeping. Today, remember that after the night of weeping, God promises a morning of rejoicing and His lasting favor.

**99. Matthew 5:9 (NIV): "Blessed are the peacemakers, for they will be called children of God."**

Peacemakers reflect God's character and are blessed. Today, strive to be a peacemaker in your interactions, promoting peace and reconciliation and living as a true child of God.

**100. Ephesians 2:8-9 (NIV): "For it is by grace you have been saved, through faith—and this is not from yourselves, it is the gift of God—not by works, so that no one can boast."**

Salvation is a gift of grace through faith, not by works. Today, rejoice in the grace of God that saves you, and live humbly, knowing that His gift, not your effort, brings salvation.

**101. Psalm 103:12 (NIV): "As far as the east is from the we, so far has he removed our transgressions from us."**

God's forgiveness obliterates our sins. Today, accept God's forgiveness and live in the freedom from knowing your sins are removed far from you.

**102. James 1:5 (NIV): "If any of you lacks wisdom, you should ask God, who gives generously to all without finding fault, and it will be given to you."**

God generously provides wisdom to those who ask. Today, seek God's wisdom in all your decisions, trusting He will generously give it to you and guide you with His perfect knowledge.

**103. Psalm 23:5 (NIV): "You prepare a table before me in the presence of my enemies. You anoint my head with oil; my cup overflows."**

God's provision and blessing overflow in our lives, even in the presence of enemies. Today, trust in God's abundant provision and blessing, knowing He prepares a table for you and anoints you with His favor.

**104. Hebrews 11:1 (NIV): "Now faith is confidence in what we hope for and assurance about what we do not see."**

Faith gives us confidence and assurance in what we hope for, even without seeing it. Today, strengthen your faith, trust God's promises, and have confidence in His unseen work.

**105. Psalm 9:9 (NIV): "The Lord is a refuge for the oppressed, a stronghold in times of trouble."**

God is a refuge and stronghold for the oppressed. Today, seek refuge in the Lord, knowing He is your stronghold and protector in times of trouble.

**106. Romans 8:32 (NIV): "He who did not spare his own Son, but gave him up for us all—how will he not also, along with him, graciously give us all things?"**

God's willingness to give His Son assures us of His generosity in giving us all things. Today, trust in God's provision and generosity, knowing He will graciously provide for all your needs.

**107. Psalm 37:3 (NIV): "Trust in the Lord and do good; dwell in the land and enjoy safe pasture."**

Trusting in the Lord and doing good brings safety and provision. Today, trust God, do good to others, and enjoy the security and provision of living in His care.

**108. 1 John 3:1 (NIV): "See what great love the Father**

**has lavished on us, that we should be called children of God! And that is what we are!"**

God's great love makes us His children. Today, rejoice in your identity as a child of God, embracing His lavish love and sharing it with others.

**109. Psalm 73:26 (NIV): "My flesh and my heart may fail, but God is the strength of my heart and my portion forever."**

God is our strength and portion, even when our flesh and heart fail. Today, rely on God's strength to sustain you, knowing He is your eternal portion and support.

**110. Philippians 4:8 (NIV): "Finally, brothers and sisters, whatever is true, whatever is noble, whatever is right, whatever is pure, whatever is lovely, whatever is admirable—if anything is excellent or praiseworthy— think about such things."**

Focusing on what is true, noble, correct, pure, lovely, admirable, excellent, and praiseworthy brings peace and positivity. Today, fill your mind with these things, aligning your thoughts with God's goodness.

**111. Psalm 119:11 (NIV): "I have hidden your word in my heart that I might not sin against you."**

Hiding God's Word in our hearts helps us avoid sin. Today, commit to memorizing and meditating on Scripture, allowing it to guide your actions and keep you from sinning.

**112. Romans 5:3-4 (NIV): "Not only so, but we also glory in our sufferings, because we know that suffering produces perseverance; perseverance, character; and character, hope."**

Suffering produces perseverance, character, and hope. Today, view your trials as opportunities for growth, knowing that God is developing perseverance, character, and hope in you through your challenges.

**113. Psalm 18:32 (NIV): "It is God who arms me with strength and keeps my way secure."**

God arms us with strength and secures our way. Today, rely on God's strength to equip you for every challenge, trusting He will keep your path secure.

**114. 2 Timothy 4:7 (NIV): "I have fought the good fight, I have finished the race, I have kept the faith."**

Completing our spiritual race with faithfulness brings fulfillment. Today, commit to fighting the good fight, finishing your race, and keeping the faith, knowing that God's reward awaits you.

**115. Ephesians 4:32 (NIV): "Be kind and compassionate to one another, forgiving each other, just as in Christ God forgave you."**

Kindness, compassion, and forgiveness reflect Christ's love. Today, practice these virtues in your relationships, forgiving others as God has forgiven you and showing kindness and compassion in all your interactions.

**116. Psalm 34:1 (NIV): "I will extol the Lord at all times; his praise will always be on my lips."**

Praising the Lord at all times keeps our focus on His goodness. Today, make it a habit to praise God continually, letting His praise always be on your lips, no matter the circumstances.

**117. Romans 8:31 (NIV): "What, then, shall we say in response to these things? If God is for us, who can be against us?"**

God's support makes us victorious over opposition. Today, find confidence in knowing that God is for you and that no opposition can stand against His power and support in your life.

**118. Psalm 145:18 (NIV): "The Lord is near to all who call on him, to all who call on him in truth."**

God is near to those who call on Him in truth. Today, approach God with sincerity and truth, knowing He is close and ready to listen to your prayers.

**119. Philippians 2:14-15 (NIV): "Do everything without grumbling or arguing, so that you may become blameless and pure, 'children of God without fault in a warped and crooked generation.' Then you will shine among them like stars in the sky."**

Living without grumbling or arguing sets us apart as God's children. Today, strive to do everything positively, avoid complaints and arguments, and shine as a light in a dark world.

**120. 2 Corinthians 1:3-4 (NIV): "Praise be to the God and Father of our Lord Jesus Christ, the Father of compassion and the God of all comfort, who comforts us in all our troubles, so that we can comfort those in any trouble with the comfort we ourselves receive from God."**

God's comfort enables us to comfort others. Today, receive God's comfort in your troubles and extend that comfort to those around you, sharing His compassion and care.

**121. Psalm 62:6 (NIV): "Truly he is my rock and my salvation; he is my fortress, I will not be shaken."**

God's steadfastness makes us unshakable. Today, anchor yourself in God's strength and salvation, trusting He is your unmovable rock and fortress.

**122. James 5:16 (NIV): "Therefore confess your sins to each other and pray for each other so that you may be healed. The prayer of a righteous person is powerful and effective."**

Confession and prayer bring healing and effectiveness. Today, practice confessing your sins and praying for others, knowing that your prayers as a righteous person are powerful and effective.

**123. John 14:6 (NIV): "Jesus answered, 'I am the way and the truth and the life. No one comes to the Father except through me.'"**

Jesus is the only way to the Father. Today, reaffirm your faith in Jesus as the way, the truth, and the life, and share this truth with others, pointing them to the path of salvation.

**124. Psalm 31:24 (NIV): "Be strong and take heart, all you who hope in the Lord."**

Hoping in the Lord gives us strength and courage. Today, be strong and take heart, placing your hope firmly in the Lord and finding the strength to face any challenges that come your way.

**125. Romans 8:37 (NIV): "No, in all these things we are more than conquerors through him who loved us."**

Through Christ's love, we are more than conquerors. Today, live with the confidence that you are victorious in Christ, overcoming all challenges and obstacles through His love and power.

**126. Psalm 91:1 (NIV): "Whoever dwells in the shelter of the Most High will rest in the shadow of the Almighty."**

Dwelling in God's presence brings rest and peace. Today, make it your goal to dwell in the shelter of the Most High, finding rest and security in His almighty shadow.

**127. Hebrews 13:8 (NIV): "Jesus Christ is the same yesterday and today and forever."**

Jesus' unchanging nature gives us stability and assurance. Today, take comfort in the constancy of Jesus, knowing that He is the same yesterday, today, and forever, and His promises remain steadfast.

**128. 2 Corinthians 9:7 (NIV): "Each of you should give what you have decided in your heart to give, not reluctantly or under compulsion, for God loves a cheerful giver."**

God loves cheerful giving from the heart. Today, give generously and cheerfully, knowing that your giving pleases God and reflects His generosity.

# ABOUT THE AUTHOR

Elliott Middleton, Ph. D., is a former decision scientist and college professor who has built risk models for JP Morgan Chase, UBS, and other large financial institutions. His work on confidence levels in the economy has been quoted in *The Wall Street Journal* and *ZeroHedge*. He lives with his family in the Nashville, Tennessee, area.